Navigating Networks:

A Comprehensive Guide to IPv4 Addressing for Tech Enthusiasts, CCNA Candidates, and Networking Professionals

Copyright Page

including but not limited to, any direct, indirect, incidental, consequential, special, or exemplary damages arising from or in connection with the use of this book or its information.

Published by Kevogo Musudia

Who Is This Book For?

The book is carefully crafted to be useful to a wide range of readers. It mostly serves aspirant tech professionals who are looking to gain a solid understanding of IPv4 addressing as a fundamental skill in networking. The book is a priceless tool for those getting ready to master the challenges of IP addressing on their certification journey, with a specific focus on helping CCNA exam candidates. Even educators and IT decision-makers can gain insights from the book to improve their teaching strategies or make wise decisions about network infrastructure. Through a well-crafted blend of theoretical explanations and practical exercises, the book provides practical insights for network enthusiasts, beginners, self-learners, and experienced IT professionals looking to bolster their understanding of this critical networking aspect.

What can you expect?

This book's goal is to provide a wide variety of skills and knowledge that are specifically suited to each reader. Aspiring IT professionals will develop a thorough understanding of IP addressing, subnetting, and associated networking ideas, putting them on the road to becoming knowledgeable network practitioners. They will discover how devices communicate within a network as well as the construction of IP addresses, the significance of subnetting, and more. Candidates for the CCNA exam will be prepared with an in-depth understanding of IPv4 addressing, a critical subject in the test. Candidates will gain confidence in handling subnetting questions, a substantial section of the CCNA exam.

A solid understanding of Troubleshooting common IP addressing issues is critical and a crucial component of CCNA certification. The book simplifies complicated networking ideas for beginners and network enthusiasts into explanations that are simple to understand, giving it a great place to start for those with little to no background knowledge and promoting more accessible learning. To participate in conversations and learn more about networking, they will become more conversant with the language used in networking. Professionals and self-learners will have a complete understanding of IP addressing, filling up any knowledge gaps. Professionals can apply their newly acquired knowledge to actual networking difficulties by using real-world situations and exercises. Teachers, educators, and instructors can use the book's well-organized content to improve their course materials and make sure that students thoroughly understand the IP addressing. The information required to make wise judgments on network design, addressing schemes, and security issues will be acquired by IT Managers and Decision Makers. Managers can interact with their technical teams and outside partners more successfully by having a deeper understanding of IPv4 addressing.

Why IP Addressing?

IP addressing is the fundamental building block of contemporary communication, allowing devices to identify, find, and exchange data in real time across networks. Understanding IP addressing is similar to having the key that unlocks the possibility of network management and troubleshooting in this digital age, where interconnection is at the core of business, communication, and daily life.

The foundation of networking understanding is IP addressing. It gives the ability to build organized, effective networks that make it easier to share resources and transmit data. This book allows easy comprehension of IP addressing completely, enabling beginners to confidently negotiate the challenges of network design.

The concepts of Subnetting and IP addressing are heavily emphasized in the CCNA test, a prestigious credential in the networking field. "Navigating Networks" guarantees participants' success in this exam domain and gives them the practical knowledge they need to successfully address real-world networking difficulties.

Ipv4 addresses the importance of identifying and resolving network problems is also highlighted in the book. A sound knowledge of IPv4 addressing provides the foundation for all of these duties, whether one is setting devices, controlling network traffic, or implementing security protocols.

In conclusion, the "Navigating Networks" book emphasizes how important IP addressing is in networking environments. It turns beginners into skilled tech professionals and test takers, empowering them to build reliable networks, succeed on certification examinations, and effectively negotiate the challenging landscape of contemporary networking. This book is a lot more than a how-to manual; it serves as a springboard for maximizing IP addressing's potential and advancing one's career in networking.

Table of Contents

Chapter 1: Introduction to IPv4 Addressing

IPv4 addressing is the foundation of modern networking, it is examined in depth in this chapter. It is the primary protocol used for identifying and locating devices on the local area network, intranet, extranet, and the internet, it is essential knowledge for aspiring computer professionals and those getting ready for the CCNA exam. There are still numerous networks that use IPv4 addressing today, even though the businesses that use them are moving to IPv6. Therefore, it is still essential for a student to possess a thorough knowledge of IPv4 addressing. In this module, the fundamental ideas of IPv4 addressing are explained in great detail. We start by going through the significance of IP addressing in the context of networking and demonstrating how it makes it easier for connected devices to communicate and transfer data. Next, we go into IPv4, dissecting its design and studying the components that go into an IP address. By the end of this chapter, you will be well-versed in IPv4 addressing, setting the foundation for a complete awareness of its complexity and applications throughout the rest of this book.

1.1 Importance of IP addressing

Anyone entering the networking industry or pursuing a career in technology must understand IP addressing. It is fundamental to how gadgets connect and exchange messages with one another. IP addresses ensure that data packets are accurately routed to their intended destinations across networks, just like physical addresses make it possible for mail to be delivered to the correct spot. It acts as a distinctive identification for each networked device, including computers, smartphones, and other devices. It facilitates data transmission and reception, resource access, and device-to-device communication through local networks and the public network.

You can efficiently configure and administer networks if you understand IP addresses. Using this knowledge, you may distribute and give devices IP addresses for each to have a unique identity on the network. Networking technologies including subnetting, routing, and network address translation (NAT) all have their roots in IP addressing. It is difficult to debug network problems, create scalable networks, or implement advanced networking features without a solid understanding of IP addressing.

In conclusion, being aware of the significance of IP addressing equips you with the skills needed to efficiently build, operate, and troubleshoot networks. It gives you the ability to manage the complexities of networking technology, facilitating easy data transmission and communication between devices in the networked digital environment.

1.2 Role of IPv4 in Networking

An essential protocol for computer networks, Internet Protocol version 4 (IPv4) enables data transport and communication between devices. It acts as the standard protocol for allocating addresses to and directing data packets over the internet.32-bit numbers make up IPv4 addresses commonly written in the form of dotted decimals (for example, 192.168.0.1), giving each networked device a special identification number.

The importance of IPv4 in networking cannot be overstated. Devices may connect, exchange data, and access resources across connected networks thanks to it. By allocating distinct addresses for each device on a network, IPv4 addressing makes it easier for data packets to be sent from a source device to a destination device. This addressing scheme uses routing protocols and networking tools like routers to make sure that data gets to the intended recipient.

Through the use of subnets, IPv4 also provides network segmentation and structure. Subnetting is a technique that divides a network into smaller logical subnetworks to effectively distribute IP addresses and improve network management and security.

Additionally, IPv4 is crucial for network security. IPv4 addressing is used by firewalls and access control lists (ACLs) to manage network traffic, enforce security guidelines, and defend against unwanted access and malicious activity.

Despite its importance, IPv4 has problems because there are only a small number of addresses (around 4.3 billion) accessible. Internet Protocol version 6 (IPv6), which offers a bigger address space to meet the rising needs of the internet, was adopted due to the IPv4 address exhaustion caused by the quick expansion of internet-connected devices.

Despite this, IPv4 is still widely used and serves as the foundation of many networks. To configure, maintain, and troubleshoot networks efficiently, network administrators and aspiring tech professionals alike must understand IPv4 and its function in networking.

1.3 The structure of IPv4 addresses

Each computer on a network is given an IP address, which is a numerical identity. It indicates a device's precise location on the network. Regardless of the LAN type, the hosts are a part of, it enables communication between hosts on different networks. The three techniques listed below are commonly used to represent IP addresses:

1. Decimal such as:172.16.10.5
2. Binary such as:10101100.00010000.00011110.00111000
3. Hexadecimal such as:c0a8:d554

IPv4 addresses have a specified structure that consists of four octets (groups of numbers) separated by periods. The full address consists of 32 bits because each octet represents 8 bits. The network is always identified in the first part. The host is named in the final part. Data packets may be effectively understood and routed by devices thanks to the address' binary representation.

Here is an illustration of how IPv4 addresses are structured:

Illustration I

IP Address:10.0.0.50

Subnet mask:255.0.0.0

The IPv4 address in this illustration has four octets, 10, 0, 0, and 50.

Let's analyze each octet in turn:

Octet 1: 10

Binary code: 00001010

Identifies the address's network portion.

Octet 2: 0

Binary code: 00000000

Identifies the address's host portion.

Octet 3: 0

Binary code: 00000000

Identifies the address's host portion.

Octet 4: 50.

Binary code: 00110010

Identifies the address's host portion.

The network portion in this case is represented by the first octet (10), whereas the host portion is represented by the next three octets (0.0.50). The way the network is divided into its network and host components relies on the subnet mask used.

For subnetting, addressing distribution, and configuring network hardware like routers and firewalls, it is crucial to comprehend the structure of IPv4 addresses. It allows easy management and troubleshooting of networks effectively, ensuring effective data routing and device connectivity.

Illustration II

IP Address:192.168.0.1

Subnet mask:255.255.255.0

Four octets make up the IPv4 address in this instance: 192, 168, 0, and 1. Let's dissect each octet to see what it means:

Octet 1: 192

Binary code: 11000000

Identifies the address's network portion.

Octet 2: 168

Binary code: 10101000

Identifies the address's network portion.

Octet 3: 0

Binary code: 00000000

Identifies the address's network portion.

Octet 4: 1.

Binary code: 00000001

Identifies the address's host portion.

The first three octets in this example (192.168.0) stand for the network portion, whereas the other octets (1) stand for the host portion. The subnet mask determines how the network and host components are separated.

1.4 The concept of a subnet mask

A subnet mask in IPv4 addressing is a 32-bit value that separates an IP address into the network portion and the host portion. It chooses how many bits from the IP address should be allotted to the network and how many for the host.

Let's revisit the earlier example of the IP address 192.168.0.1 and the network mask 255.255.255.0 to gain a better understanding of subnet masks. The subnet mask has a similar dotted decimal representation to IP addresses, but it has a different function.

The subnet mask is made up of a string of consecutive 1s and consecutive 0s. In this instance, the binary representation of the subnet mask 255.255.255.0 is as follows:

11111111.11111111.11111111.00000000

The subnet mask's ones and zeros stand for the host and network portions, respectively. In this instance, the network is given the first 24 bits (3 bytes), and the host is given the final 8 bits (1 byte).

You can perform a bitwise logical AND operation using the above example between the IP address and subnet mask taking note of the network as follows:

Host Address	192	168	0	1
Subnet Mask	255	255	255	0
Host address in binary	11000000	10101000	00000000	00000001
Subnet Mask in binary	11111111	11111111	11111111	00000000
Network Address in binary	11000000	10101000	00000000	00000000
Network Address in decimal	192	168	0	0

By keeping the bits in the IP address that match the ones in the subnet mask and setting all other bits to zero, the network address can be derived. The network address in this instance is 192.168.0.0.

The network's devices are represented by the host component of the IP address. In this illustration, the host address is represented by the eighth and last byte (0000001) of the IP address. The range of valid host addresses within this subnet would be from 192.168.0.1 to 192.168.0.254 because the host portion can have 28 (256) different values. The network address (192.168.1.0) and the broadcast address (192.168.1.255) are the only addresses in the subnet that are reserved.

You can utilize IP addresses more effectively by being divided into smaller subnetworks thanks to subnet masks. Organizations can build numerous subnets with unique host address ranges throughout a single network by employing various subnet masks. To ensure proper routing and communication, it's crucial to note that subnet masks should be properly established on all devices inside a network

Review Exercise

Determine the host address in binary, the subnet mask in binary, and the network address in decimal for each of the given IPv4 addresses by analyzing the table below.

	IP Address	Subnet Mask	Host Address in binary	Subnet Mask in binary
1.	192.168.100.10	255.255.255.0		
2.	172.16.10.50	255.255.0.0		
3.	10.0.0.9	255.0.0.0		

Solutions

Conversion of Host address to Binary

Question 1:192.168.100.10

Converting 192.168.100.10 to binary:

192 in binary is 11000000

168 in binary is 10101000

100 in binary is 01100100

10 in binary is   00001010

Now, combine all the binary octets:

192.168.100.100 in binary is: 11000000.10101000.01100100.00001010

Question 2: 172.16.10.50

Converting 172.16.10.50 to binary:

172 in binary is 1010110

16   in binary is 00010000

10   in binary is 00001010

50   in binary is 00110010

Now, combine all the binary octets:

172.16.10.50 in binary is:10101100.00010000.00001010.00110010

Question 3:10.0.0.9

Converting 10.0.0.9 to binary:

10 in binary is 00001010

0 in binary is 00000000

0 in binary is 00000000

9 in binary is 00001001

Now, combine all the binary octets:

10.0.0.9 in binary is:00001010.00000000.00000000.00001001

Conversion of Subnet Mask to Binary

Case study mask: 255.255.255.0

Converting 255.255.255.0

255 to binary is 11111111

255 in binary is 11111111

255 in binary is 11111111

0   in binary is 00000000

Now, combine all the binary octets together:

255.255.255.0 in binary is: 11111111.11111111.11111111.00000000

When   255.255.0.0   is   converted   to   binary   it   will   be:
11111111.11111111.00000000.00000000

When   255.0.0.0   is   converted   to   binary   it   will   be:
11111111.00000000.00000000.00000000

Chapter 2: Classful IP Addressing

The initial approach of categorizing version 4 (IPv4) of the Internet Protocol address space into various classes based on their leading bits is known as classful IP addressing. Five classes: Class A, Class B, Class C, Class D, and Class E were used in this scheme to categorize IP addresses. Each class has a predetermined network and host part as well as a specified range of addresses. Classful IP addressing, which offered a simple method for address assignment, was crucial in the early phases of the internet's growth. Classful addressing was, however, succeeded by CIDR, or classless inter-domain routing and subnetting techniques resulting from the expansion of both the internet and the necessity for more effective address allocation. Even though classful IP addressing is no longer commonly used in contemporary IP networks, understanding it is nevertheless crucial for basic networking knowledge and historical background.

Let's examine the classes:

2.1 Class A

The initial bit of the first byte in a Class A network must always be off, or 0 in binary notation.

The initial bit of the first byte must be between 0 to 127 represented as decimal notation.

The network address is contained in the first octet of a Class A address. The host address is in the final three octets (net. host. host. host).

We have $2^7=128$ Class A networks in existence. The reason for the seven is that the first octet has eight bits, the first of which must be "0." The remaining seven bits might be any value between 0 and 1.

There are 2^{24} hosts and 16,777,216 million IP addresses per network. The final three octets contain twenty-four bits, hence the number 24. The first and last IP addresses cannot be used as hosts, therefore the -2 takes care of the network and broadcast address. The network address is the initial address (net.0.0.0). The broadcast address is the final address (net.255.255.255).

Illustration: IP Address 10.15.30.16

10	15	30	16	Class A source address
255	0	0	0	Class A network mask
10 0	0		0	The network Portion of the address
0 16	15		30	The host portion of the address
10 1	0		0	First valid host address
10 254	255		255	The last valid host address
10 255	255		255	Broadcast address

2.2 Class B

The initial bit of the first byte in a Class B network must always be 10 in binary notation.

The initial bit of the first byte must be between 128 to 191 represented as decimal notation.

The network address is contained in the first and second octets of a Class B address. The host address is in the final two octets (net. net. host. host). We have 2^{14}=16,384 Class B networks in existence. The reason for the fourteen is that the first two octets have sixteen bits, the first of which must be "10." The remaining fourteen bits might be any value between 0 and 1.

There are 2^{16} hosts which is around 65,536 IP addresses per network. The final two octets contain sixteen bits, hence the number 16.

The first and last IP addresses cannot be used as hosts, therefore the -2 takes care of the network and broadcast address.

The network address is the initial address (net.net.0.0).

The broadcast address is the final address (net.net.255.255).

Illustration: IP Address 172.30.16.10

172	30	16	10	Class A source address
255	255	0	0	Class A network mask
172	30	0	0	The network Portion of the address
0	0	16	10	The host portion of the address
172	30	0	1	First valid host address
172	30	255	254	The last valid host address
172	30	255	255	Broadcast address

2.3 Class C

The initial bit of the first byte in a Class C network must always be 110 in binary notation.

The initial bit of the first byte must be between 192 to 223 represented as decimal notation.

The network address is contained in the first, second, and third octets of a Class C address. The host address is in the final octet (net. net. net. host).

We have $2^{21}=2,097,152$ Class C networks in existence. The reason for the twenty-one bits is that the first three octets have twenty-four bits, the first of which must be "110." The remaining twenty-one bits might be any value between 0 and 1.

There are 2^8 hosts which is around 256 IP addresses per network. The final octet contains eight bits, hence the number 8. The first and last IP addresses cannot be used as hosts, therefore the -2 takes care of the network and broadcast address.

The network address is the initial address (net.net.net.0).

The broadcast address is the final address (net.net.net.255)

Illustration: IP Address 192.168.30.16

192	168	30	16	Class C source address
255	255	255	0	Class C network mask
192	168	30	0	The network Portion of the address
0	0	0	16	The host portion of the address
192	168	30	1	First valid host address
192	168	30	254	The last valid host address

192	168	30	255	Broadcast address

2.4 Class D

As part of the IP addressing scheme's initial architecture, it was decided to reserve Class D addresses for multicast addresses. A single packet can be sent simultaneously to several locations using the networking technique known as multicast.

The requirement for effective one-to-many communication was recognized by the creators of the Internet Protocol (IP) at the time of its original development. They chose to reserve a certain range of addresses within the IP address space for multicast purposes rather than using unicast addresses (which are used for one-to-one communication) or designating a new address space for multicast.

It made it possible for multicast traffic to be handled and routed across networks effectively by setting aside Class D addresses for it. The reserved Class D address range (224.0.0.0 to 239.255.255.255) can be used by routers and networking equipment to recognize and properly handle multicast packets.

By ensuring that multicast communication is easily identifiable and can be effectively routed to the intended receivers, using a dedicated address range for multicast simplifies the network infrastructure. Network administrators can distribute multicast addresses inside this restricted range without worrying about issues with unicast or other addressing systems.

It's important to remember that CIDR, or Classless Inter-Domain Routing has largely replaced the idea of classful addressing, especially Class D. Without the limitations imposed by the classful addressing scheme, CIDR later discussed in this book permits a more flexible allocation of addresses, including the allocation of multicast addresses.

2.5 Class E

Class E address was initially intended for testing with a range (240.0.0.0 to 255.255.255.254) created. To let businesses, researchers, and developers test out new networking technologies, protocols, and applications without interfering with the IP backbone, this range was set aside for reserved use.

The goal was to establish an IP address space "playground" for experimentation and innovation. Class E addresses weren't ever meant to be allocated or used widely in production networks.

It's crucial to remember that, contrary to initial expectations, the Class E range has not been extensively employed for experimental purposes in actuality. Instead, the range has not been widely adopted or allocated and is mainly seen as "reserved for future use".

The entire Class E address space has been declared as "reserved" in modern networking, and IANA (Internet Assigned Numbers Authority) advises against using it in any IP network. This recommendation was made due to the possibility of problems with upcoming IP protocols or standards as well as the limited availability of Class E addresses in networking hardware.

Overall, even though Class E addresses were initially designed for experimental uses, they haven't been actively allocated or used in actual networks, and their reserved status inhibits their use.

2.6 IPv4 addresses with special uses

Even in the current era of IP addressing employing CIDR, or Classless Inter-Domain Routing, some addresses, such as the network address, broadcast address, and loopback address, cannot be given to hosts as unicast addresses. Let's attempt to understand every single one of them.

Network address

The precise address that identifies a network or subnet is referred to as a network address. It is essential for routing and communication between various networks and aids in determining the network part of an IP address. Applying the "bitwise AND" logical operation between the IP address and the matching subnet mask yields the network address.

Let's use an example to demonstrate this:

Example:

IP Address: 192.168.0.10

Subnet Mask: 255.255.255.0

In this case, we have an IP address of 192.168.0.10 and a subnet mask of 255.255.255.0. We use the bitwise AND operation between the IP address and the subnet mask to find the network address:

IP Address: 11000000.10101000.00000000.00001010

Subnet Mask: 11111111.11111111.11111111. 00000000

Network Address: 11000000.10101000.00000000.00000000 (192.168.0.0)

The network address in this instance is 192.168.0.0. It indicates which network IP address 192.168.0.10 is a part of. When deciding how to forward packets within a network, routers consult the network address, which denotes the network's origin.

It's crucial to remember that the network address can only be used to identify the network as a whole; it cannot be used to identify specific sites inside the network. The host part of an IP address, which is created by changing the network bits to 0, helps identify specific networked devices. Routing decisions depend on network addresses. Routers utilize the network address to decide which route is the best path to take when a packet is transmitted from one network to another. The absence of the network address would prevent routers from identifying the destination network, which would prevent the packet from reaching its intended location.

The identification of networks or subnets, the facilitation of routing selections, and the permitting of communication between various networks are all important functions of network addresses in IP networking.

Broadcast address

A broadcast address permits a packet to be sent to every device on a specific network or subnet. All hosts on that network receive packets sent to the broadcast address, making it possible to communicate effectively with many devices at once.

Let's use an example to demonstrate this:

Example:

Network Address: 192.168.0.0

Subnet Mask: 255.255.255.0

The network address in this example is 192.168.0.0, and the subnet mask is 255.255.255.0. By turning all host bits of an IP address to 1 inside the network range, the broadcast address can be found. We use the bitwise OR operation to combine the network address with the bitwise complement of the subnet mask to determine the broadcast address:

Network Address: 11000000.10101000.00000000.00000000 (192.168.0.0)

Subnet Mask: 11111111.11111111.11111111. 00000000

Bitwise Complement: 00000000.00000000.00000000.11111111

Broadcast Address: 11000000.10101000.00000000.11111111 (192.168.0.255)

The broadcast address in this instance is 192.168.0.255. A packet sent to this address will be transmitted to every device connected to the 192.168.0.0 network. This is beneficial in circumstances where a message or piece of data needs to be sent concurrently to several hosts on the same network.

A device understands that a packet addressed to the broadcast address is intended for all other devices on the network and processes it accordingly when it receives it. For instance, based on the received packet, a device might respond to a broadcast message or update its network information. It's crucial to remember that a broadcast address is unique to a certain network or subnet. Each network will have its unique broadcast address.

Since the goal of broadcast packets is to reach every device on a local network, routers normally do not forward them to other networks.

Overall, by enabling effective communication with several devices inside a network at once, the broadcast address plays a significant part in IP networking. It permits the distribution of packets to every host connected to a network, which facilitates complete activities like service discovery, resource sharing, and network-wide announcements.

Loopback address

A device can send network traffic to itself using a loopback address, a special IP address that does not require physical network interfaces or other external networks. Testing, troubleshooting, and contact with the local host are frequently carried out through it.

It is more typical to merely refer to loopback addresses as 127.0.0.1 though the range is (127.0.0.0 /8 or 127.0.0.1 to 127.255.255.254). The virtual network interface known as the loopback network interface, which is present on every device and is used to transmit and receive data within the local host, is given this task.

To get the idea of a loopback address, let's look at an illustration:

Example:

Loopback Address: 127.0.0.1

The loopback address in this illustration is 127.0.0.1, which is the typical IPv4 loopback address. When a device transmits packets to this address, those packets are internally looped back and sent to that device's network stack.

For instance, if a computer application sends a packet to the loopback address 127.0.0.1, the network stack of the same device receives it right away without having to pass through any actual network interfaces or leave the local machine. This enables communication with services running on the local host or testing network functioning and connection.

```
Microsoft Windows [Version 10.0.19045.4412]
(c) Microsoft Corporation. All rights reserved.

C:\Users\KM-PC>ping 127.0.0.1

Pinging 127.0.0.1 with 32 bytes of data:
Reply from 127.0.0.1: bytes=32 time<1ms TTL=128
Reply from 127.0.0.1: bytes=32 time<1ms TTL=128
Reply from 127.0.0.1: bytes=32 time<1ms TTL=128
Reply from 127.0.0.1: bytes=32 time<1ms TTL=128

Ping statistics for 127.0.0.1:
    Packets: Sent = 4, Received = 4, Lost = 0 (0% loss),
Approximate round trip times in milli-seconds:
    Minimum = 0ms, Maximum = 0ms, Average = 0ms
```

The loopback address is frequently employed in several circumstances, including:

Local Testing: Without relying on external networks, developers frequently test an application's network-related features using the loopback address. This makes it possible to isolate and test network capabilities on the same device.

Troubleshooting: Technicians and Network administrators can utilize the local machine's loopback address to identify and resolve network-related problems. They can test the functionality of the network stack and related services by sending packets to the loopback address.

Communication between services: Using the loopback address, services running on the same machine can talk to one another. The loopback address, for instance, might be used by a web server operating on a computer to communicate with a database that is hosted locally or with other services.

It's vital to remember that the loopback address does not use any external networks and may only be accessed from the same device. It is not utilized for network connection among various gadgets.

The loopback address is generally a helpful tool for local testing, troubleshooting, and internal host communication. Without the requirement for external connectivity, it enables network traffic to be sent to and received from the same device, easing some network-related processes.

Public and Private address

The two types of IPv4 addresses are public and private. An IP address's reach and usability within a network or the Internet are specified by these criteria.

IPv4 Public Address: An Internet address that is globally unique and routable is known as a public IPv4 address. Internet Service Providers (ISPs) assign these addresses, which are then used to locate and contact Internet-connected devices. Devices can be directly accessed from other devices and networks on the Internet thanks to public IP addresses.

Example:

Public IP Address: 196.61.52.39

An example of a public IPv4 address is 196.61.52.39 here. Devices connected to the Internet can access this address since it is distinct. Servers, websites, and other devices that must be reachable from anywhere on the Internet utilize public IP addresses.

Private IPv4 Address: A private IPv4 address is used in private networks and is not globally unique. These addresses are set aside for internal use, and the Internet cannot access them directly. Private IP addresses allow devices to communicate with one another within a private network, but NAT is required for them to access the Internet.

Three private IP address ranges have been designated:

10.0.0.0 to 10.255.255.255 (10.0.0.0/8)

172.16.0.0 to 172.31.255.255 (172.16.0.0/12)

192.168.0.0 to 192.168.255.255 (192.168.0.0/16)

Example:

Private IP Address: 192.168.0.10

In this instance, 192.168.0.10 serves as a private IPv4 address. Private IP addresses are often used in LANs, LANs in offices, and residential networks. Private IP addresses enable communication between devices connected to the same private network. However, private IP addresses are converted to public IP addresses using NAT, which is carried out by routers or firewalls, to access resources on the Internet.

Because they are not directly accessible from the Internet, private IP addresses offer a certain amount of network protection. They eliminate the requirement for separate public IP addresses for every device in a private network by allowing several devices to use a single public IP address.

It's crucial to remember that private IP addresses cannot be directly utilized to connect with devices on a public network. For users to access resources on the Internet, Network Address Translation (NAT) transforms private IP addresses into the public IP address provided to the router or gateway.

Overall, the accessibility and global uniqueness of IPv4 addresses serve as a distinction between public and private addresses. While private addresses are intended for internal networks and cannot be routable on the Internet, public addresses can be routable and are used for external communication.

Review Exercise

1. Determine the type of address (network, host, multicast, broadcast, or reserved address) by analyzing the table below. An illustration of how the table should be filled out may be seen in the first row.

IP Address	Subnet Mask	Address type
172.30.10.1	255.255.0.0	Host
10.2.2.0	255.255.255.0	Network
224.10.11.56	255.255.255.0	Multicast address
192.168.50.100	255.255.255.0	Host
172.16.10.10	255.255.0.0	Host
240.192.1.100	255.252.0.0	Reserved
10.255.255.255	255.0.0.0	Broadcast

Let's figure out the way 10.2.2.0 is considered to be a network address

Understanding the subnet:

IP Address: 10.2.2.0

Subnet Mask: 255.255.255.0

The subnet mask 255.255.255.0 indicates that the first three octets (24 bits) are for the network portion, and the last octet (8 bits) is for host addresses.

Identifying the Network Address:

The network address is the lowest in the subnet. For the subnet 10.2.2.0/24, the network address is 10.2.2.0.

Host Addresses:

Host addresses are those that can be assigned to devices within the network. In the 10.2.2.0/24 subnet, host addresses range from 10.2.2.1 to 10.2.2.254.

Given this analysis, the IP address 10.2.2.0 with the subnet mask 255.255.255.0 is identified as the network address for the subnet 10.2.2.0/24. This address cannot be assigned to a host as it represents the subnet itself.

Summary:

- ✓ 10.2.2.0: Network Address (represents the subnet)
- ✓ 10.2.2.1 - 10.2.2.254: Host Addresses (assignable to devices)
- ✓ 10.2.2.255: Broadcast Address (used to communicate with all hosts in the subnet)

Therefore, the address **10.2.2.0** is a network address.

Use the same method and analogy to find the address types 192.168.50.100 and 172.16.10.10 as host addresses.

Let's figure out the way **224.10.11.56** is considered to be a **Multicast address**

Understanding the IP address range:

IP addresses are divided into classes, with specific ranges assigned to each class. The primary classes relevant here are:

Class A: 1.0.0.0 to 126.0.0.0

Class B: 128.0.0.0 to 191.255.0.0

Class C: 192.0.0.0 to 223.255.255.0

Class D (Multicast): 224.0.0.0 to 239.255.255.255

Class E (Experimental/Reserved): 240.0.0.0 to 255.255.255.255

Identifying the IP Address Class:

The IP address 224.10.11.56 falls within the range 224.0.0.0 to 239.255.255.255, which is Class D.

Purpose of Class D Addresses:

Class D addresses are designated for multicast purposes. Multicast IP addresses are used to send data to a group of destinations simultaneously, rather than to a single destination (unicast) or all possible destinations (broadcast).

Summary:

✓ 224.10.11.56: Multicast Address (used for multicast group communication)

Therefore, the address 224.10.11.56 is categorized as a multicast address.

Let's figure out the way **240.192.1.100** is considered to be a broadcast address

Identifying the IP Address Class:

The IP address 240.192.1.100 falls within the range 240.0.0.0 to 255.255.255.255, which corresponds to Class E.

Purpose of Class E Addresses:

Class E addresses are reserved for experimental purposes. They are not used for regular network operations or assigned to hosts. These addresses are typically used for research and development. Given this analysis, the IP address 240.192.1.100 is a reserved address meant for experimental use.

Summary:

✓ 240.192.1.100: Reserved Address (used for experimental purposes)

Therefore, the address 240.192.1.100 is categorized as a reserved address.

Let's figure out the way **10.255.255.255** is considered to be a **Multicast address**

Understanding the IP address range:

The IP address 10.255.255.255 falls within the private IP address range designated by the Internet Assigned Numbers Authority (IANA).

The private IP address ranges are:

10.0.0.0 to 10.255.255.255 (Class A private range)

172.16.0.0 to 172.31.255.255 (Class B private range)

192.168.0.0 to 192.168.255.255 (Class C private range)

Identifying the IP Address Class:

The IP address 10.255.255.255 is within the Class A private range (10.0.0.0 to 10.255.255.255).

Broadcast Address in the Subnet:

In a typical Class A network with a subnet mask of 255.0.0.0, the IP address 10.255.255.255 represents the broadcast address for the 10.0.0.0/8 network. This address is used to communicate with all hosts in the network.

Given this analysis, the IP address 10.255.255.255 is a broadcast address within the private Class A range.

Summary:

- ✓ 10.255.255.255: Broadcast Address (used to communicate with all hosts in the 10.0.0.0/8 network)

Therefore, the address 10.255.255.255 is categorized as a broadcast address in the private IP range.

2. Examine the table below to determine whether the address is private or public.

IP Address	Public or Private
192.137.150.11/24	Public
172.17.10.120/16	Private
10.120.60.5/8	Private
65.105.0.15/16	Public

An IP address is a device's unique address on a network, similar to how your home address is unique in your city. It assists in determining where data should be sent and received across the internet or other networks. IP addresses are divided into two main categories: private and public.

Private IP Addresses:

These are used in private networks, such as homes, schools, and companies. They are not routable on the public internet, therefore you cannot access a private IP address directly from the internet.

There are specific ranges reserved for private IP addresses:

10.0.0.0 to 10.255.255.255

172.16.0.0 to 172.31.255.255

192.168.0.0 to 192.168.255.255

Public IP Addresses:

These are used on the public internet. Any device having a public IP address can be accessed from anywhere on the internet (with adequate permissions and security).

Analyzing 192.137.150.11/24

Now, let's check the IP address 192.137.150.11:

The address is in the format 192.137.150.11.

It does not fall within the reserved private ranges:

- ✓ It is not in 10.0.0.0 to 10.255.255.255.
- ✓ It is not in 172.16.0.0 to 172.31.255.255.
- ✓ It is not in 192.168.0.0 to 192.168.255.255.

Since 192.137.150.11 is outside all the ranges reserved for private addresses, it is a public IP address.

Conclusion

192.137.150.11/24 is considered a public IP address. This means it can be accessed over the internet, unlike private IP addresses, which are only for local networks.

IP address 192.137.150.11 is like a home with an address to which anybody in the world may send mail, and a private IP address is like an apartment number to which only those within the building (network) can send mail.

You can use the same concept to determine whether IP Address:172.17.10.120/16, 10.120.60.5/8, 10.120.60.5/8, and 65.05.0.15/16 is a Public or Private address.

Chapter 3: Subnetting IPv4 Address

3.1 Introduction to Subnetting

Subnetting, sometimes referred to as subnet division, is a method for breaking up a large network into smaller, simpler subnetworks. It's a computer networking technology used to enhance network security, performance, and address space utilization.

When allocating IP addresses, subnetting offers several advantages. Some of the main benefits are as follows:

1. Effective Allocation and Use of IP Addresses: Subnetting enables effective IP address allocation and use. You can distribute IP addresses according to the unique requirements of each subnet by segmenting a network into smaller subnets. This avoids the waste of IP addresses that would happen if all devices shared a single, expansive network.

2. Scalability: Subnetting aids in the expansion and scalability of networks. Subnetting gives an organization the freedom to assign extra IP addresses to new subnets as it grows and adds more devices or subnetworks. This enables the smooth integration of new hardware and networks without the need for a full IP address setup change.

3. Tasks related to network management are made easier by subnetting. Network administrators may easily organize and manage IP addresses inside several subnets

through subnetting. It makes it possible to organize devices logically according to their location, department, function, or any other pertinent factors. By segmenting the network, it is simpler to deploy security measures, troubleshoot network problems, and apply configuration changes to particular subnets without affecting the entire network.

4. Reduced broadcast traffic and increased network efficiency are two ways that subnetting improves network performance. Broadcast messages are sent only to certain subnets in a submitted network as opposed to the entire network. This lessens broadcast traffic and enhances the responsiveness and performance of the network as a whole.

5. Enhanced Security: By enabling network segmentation, subnetting enhances network security. You can isolate various network components and manage traffic flow between them by segmenting a network into subnets. This enables the adoption of security measures like virtual private networks (VPNs), access control lists (ACLs), and firewalls to govern traffic between subnets. Subnetting restricts unauthorized access to other areas of the network and limits the impact of security breaches on the affected subnet.

6. Increased Network Efficiency: Subnetting makes routing and addressing within a network more effective. Smaller subnets let routers make more precise routing decisions, which speeds up and improves the efficiency of data transmission. To optimize

network traffic flow, subnetting also enables the development of subnet-specific policies and routing configurations.

3.2 Binary Representation and Subnet Masks

Effective network design and management depend on binary representation and subnet masks. The foundation for representing and manipulating IP addresses and subnet masks, which are essential components in subnetting and network communication, is binary representation. The boundaries of subnets are identified by subnet masks, which are binary expressions that aid in precise network traffic routing.

Subnet masks must be represented in binary to be understood and dealt with in computer networks when IP addressing and subnetting are used. Network masks, often referred to as subnet masks, are used to distinguish between the network and host parts of an IP address. They are made up of a string of binary digits (0s and 1s) arranged in a certain manner that matches the IP address's format.

A "1" stands for the network portion and a "0" stands for the host portion in the binary encoding of subnet masks. In the subnet mask, the number of consecutive "1s" denotes the network bits, whereas the number of consecutive "0s" denotes the host bits. These bits work together to specify the size and limits of a network's subnets.

Consider the subnet mask 255.255.255.0, which is frequently used in an IPv4 network. Each octet of the subnet mask must be translated to binary to comprehend its binary representation:

The binary for 255 is 11111111.

The binary for 255 is 11111111.

The binary for 255 is 11111111.

The binary for 0   is 00000000.

We can therefore conclude, the subnet mask 255.255.255.0 is represented in binary as 11111111.11111111.11111111. 00000000. The first 24 bits, or three octets, in this instance are "1s" and represent the network portion, whereas the final 8 bits, or one octet, are "0s" and represent the host portion. Due to the first and last addresses being set aside for network and broadcast addresses, respectively, this subnet mask permits 256 distinct host addresses within each subnet (2^8 - 2).

Network managers can compute the available address space, construct subnets, define networks, and execute subnetting calculations thanks to the binary encoding of subnet masks. It is a key idea in subnetting and is essential for effective IP address distribution, network segmentation, routing, and general network design and management.

The network and host components of a subnet mask are determined as follows:

Combination of IP Address and Subnet Mask: Examine an IP address and the associated subnet mask. The IP address and subnet mask are also represented in binary.

Bitwise AND Operation: Combine the binary representations of the IP address and the subnet mask using a bitwise AND operation. Bit by bit, this process compares the matching bits from both values.

Network Address as a Result: The network address is the outcome of the bitwise AND operation. The "1s" in the resultant binary value stands in for the network portion, and the "0s" for the host portion.

Host Address Range: Invert the subnet mask (turning the "0s" to "1s" and vice versa) to find the host address range within the subnet. The resulting binary value displays the host address range that is accessible in that subnet.

Take the IP 192.168.1.100 and subnet mask 255.255.255.0 as an illustration. These values are represented by the following binary values:

IP address: 11000000.10101000.00000001.01100100

Subnet mask: 11111111.11111111.11111111. 00000000

Making use of the bitwise AND operation: IP address and Subnet mask

11000000.10101000.00000001.01100100

11111111.11111111.11111111.00000000

11000000.10101000.00000001.00000000

In this case, the network address is represented by the resultant binary number 11000000.10101000.00000001. 00000000. The last octet (8 bits) is a component of the host portion, while the first three octets (24 bits) are part of the network portion.

The possible host addresses for this subnet, which is represented by the inverted subnet mask 0.0.0.255 in binary form (00000000.00000000.00000000. 11111111), range from 0.0.0.1 through 0.0.0.254.

Network administrators can determine the network and host components of an IP address by applying the subnet mask through bitwise AND operations. This knowledge is essential for effectively managing IP address allocations, subnetting, and network traffic routing.

3.3 Classless Interdomain Routing (CIDR)

It is possible to express IP addresses and the network prefixes they are connected with clearly and flexibly using the Classless Interdomain Routing (CIDR) notation. It explains the distribution of IP address blocks and the creation of subnets. Due to its improved scalability and more effective use of IP address space, CIDR notation has replaced the outdated classful addressing method.

An IP address, a slash ("/"), and a prefix length make up the CIDR notation. The prefix length identifies the number of bits used to represent the network element of the address, while the IP address serves as the base address of the network. The remaining bits are the host portion, which is used to identify specific networked devices.

The CIDR notation has the following general format:

IP_address/prefix_length

Let's dissect the elements of the CIDR notation using an example IP address:**192.168.10.0/24**

IP_address: This is the network's primary IP address. The IP address used in the example above is 192.168.10.0.

Prefix Length: The prefix length specifies the number of bits that make up the network component of the address. The prefix length used in this illustration is 24.

Looking at the IP address in binary format can help us understand the prefix length. The binary form IP address for 192.168.10.0 is:11000000.10101000.00001010.00000000

The prefix length of 24 denotes that the network portion is represented by the first 24 bits, while the host portion is represented by the final 8 bits. The last octet (8 bits) can be used to address specific hosts within the network in this situation, where the first three octets (24 bits) are fixed for the network portion.

Let's examine the CIDR notation's ability to represent various network sizes:

/32: This designates a single host address. For instance, 192.168.10.15/32 designates a single host with the IP address 192.168.10.15.

/24: This is an illustration of a network having 256 IP addresses (2^8). The network is represented by the first three octets, while host addresses are contained in the last octet. 192.168.10.0/24, for instance, denotes a network with addresses from 192.168.10.1 to 192.168.10.254.

/16: This is an illustration of a network having 65,536 IP addresses (2^{16}). The network is represented by the first two octets, while host addresses are contained in the last two octets. 192.168.0.0/16, for instance, denotes a network with addresses from 192.168.0.1 to 192.168.255.254

/8: This is an illustration of a network having 16,777,216 IP addresses (2^{24}). The network is represented by the first octet, while host addresses are contained in the last three octets. 10.0.0.0/8, for instance, denotes a network with addresses from 10.0.0.1 to 10.255.255.254

The classful addressing system is less flexible than CIDR notation, which supports varying subnet sizes. Effective IP address allocation, subnetting, and routing table aggregation are crucial for modern networking to guarantee the internet's scalability and continued expansion.

3.4 Subnetting Techniques and Calculation

Network administrators can build and optimize network designs, allocate IP addresses wisely, and improve network performance using subnetting techniques and computations. Network specialists may design reliable and scalable networks by mastering subnetting procedures, such as figuring out the necessary number of subnets and hosts, computing subnet masks and network addresses, and knowing subnetting regulations and principles. You will be able to design networks with a clear structure that adheres to the demands of their businesses.

3.4.1 Subnetting using fixed-length subnet masks (FLSM)

A subnetting approach known as fixed-length subnet mask subnetting (FLSM) involves segmenting a network into subnets, each of which has a defined number of hosts. In FLSM, there is a fixed number of hosts per subnet since the subnet mask is constant across all subnets in a network. **The approach entails dividing the host identifier to get the subnet number.**

Let's walk through an illustration of how to use FLSM for subnetting.

Case study:

A network address of 192.168.10.0 has a subnet mask of 255.255.255.0. The instructions state that 16 subnets must be created. To handle these subnets, we must decide how many bits in the subnet mask should be set aside, and find the increment depending on the least significant bit.

Step 1: Determine the number of bits required for the network portion

We must determine the smallest power of 2 that is higher than or equal to 16 so that we can

support 16 subnets.

In this instance, the smallest power of 2 that satisfies the criterion is $2^4(16)$. As a result, 4 bits must be set aside for the network part.

Step 2: Determine the number of bits available for the host portion

We deduct the number of bits set aside for the network section from the total number of host bits to get the number of bits that are available for the host portion. The subnet mask given (255.255.255.0) in binary will be 11111111.11111111.11111111. 0000000. The host portion of the address is 8 bits. In this case, 8 - 4 = 4 bits are available for the host portion.

Step 3: Calculate the number of hosts per subnet

We can determine the number of hosts per subnet using the formula 2^m - 2, where 'm' stands for the number of bits available for the host portion. In our case, each subnet will support 2^4-2 = 14 hosts.

Step 4: Determine network increment based on the least significant bit

The rightmost bit in an IP address's binary representation is the least significant. From the previous steps we reserved 4 bits for the network portion, The least significant bit to form a subnet number increment of one network to another will be the fourth bit starting with 1 as a binary or 128 as a decimal.

In this case, we have 11110000 as a binary and when converted to decimal will be 128 64 32 16.

To find the increment, we look at the value represented by the least significant bit which in this case will be 16

Step 5: Determine Multiple Networks and Subnet mask

To get subnets, utilize the increment, in this case, 16, with the lowest network provided, which was 192.168.10.0, to determine subsequent networks.

From this perspective, the first five networks are:

192.168.10.0

192.168.10.16

192.168.10.32

192.168.10.48

192.168.10.64

To find the subnet mask, we begin with a default subnet mask of 32 bits and designate the reserved bits for the network portion to define the subnet mask. The subnet mask in this example will be 255.255.255.240 (or /28 in CIDR notation) since we need to spare 4 bits for the network part on the last octet.

As a result, the networks will be depicted as:

192.168.10.0   /28 or 255.255.255.240

192.168.10.16   /28 or 255.255.255.240

192.168.10.32   /28 or 255.255.255.240

192.168.10.48   /28 or 255.255.255.240

192.168.10.64   /28 or 255.255.255.240

As an example, let's use 192.168.10.0/28. The first, last, and broadcast addresses will be as follows:

Network:192.168.10.0

First:192.168.10.1

Last:192.168.10.14

Broadcast:192.168.10.15

It's vital to remember that the broadcast address is always considered to be the number before the following network. Alternatively, you can take the network address and add the increment less 1

3.4.2 Variable-length subnet masks (VLSM)

With the use of the subnetting technique known as variable length subnet masking (VLSM), network managers can designate multiple sizes for their subnets, each of which can contain a varied number of hosts. In contrast to Fixed Length Subnet Masking (FLSM), which ensures that every subnet has the same number of hosts, VLSM optimizes IP address allocation, minimizing address waste and promoting more effective utilization of IP address space.

Let's use the following situation to illustrate VLSM computation:

Case study

Let's say a business' internal network has been given the IP address range 192.168.10.0/24. Three departments within the business have various demands regarding the number of hosts in each subnet:

1. Marketing Department: Needs up to 50 host addresses.
2. HR Department: Needs up to 25 host addresses.
3. Finance Department: Needs up to 10 host addresses.
4. IT department: Needs up to 6 host addresses

Step 1: Sort the departments in ascending or descending order according to the needs of their hosts:

1. Marketing Department: Needs up to 50 host addresses. (Largest)
2. HR Department: Needs up to 25 host addresses.
3. Finance Department: Needs up to 10 host addresses.
4. IT department: Needs up to 6 host addresses. (smallest)

Step 2: Determine the number of bits required for the host portion

The Marketing Department requires up to 50 hosts. We must determine the smallest power of 2 that is higher than or equal to 50 so that we can support 50 hosts.

In this instance, the smallest power of 2 that satisfies the criterion is 2^6(64). As a result, 6 bits must be set aside for the host portion of the address.

From the subnet mask given, /24 or 255.255.255.0 as a binary 11111111.11111111.11111111. 00000000 when 6 bits are reserved it will be 11111111.11111111.11111111.11000000 or /26.

We can confidently state that a subnet size of /26, which provides for 64 addresses and (2^6 - 2 = 62 usable addresses), can accommodate at least 50 hosts.

From the network given the first two subnets based on the increment will be:

192.168.10.0/26

192.168.10.64/26

The next subnet in this regard must start from 192.168.10.64/26 with the next available CIDR value

HR Department requires up to 25 hosts. We must determine the smallest power of 2 that is higher than or equal to 25 so that we can support 25 hosts.

In this instance, the smallest power of 2 that satisfies the criterion is 2^5(32). As a result, 5 bits must be set aside for the host portion of the address.

From the subnet mask given, /24 or 255.255.255.0 as a binary 11111111.11111111.11111111. 00000000 when 5 bits are reserved it will be 11111111.11111111.11111111.11100000 or /27.

We can confidently state that a subnet size of /27, which provides for 32 addresses and (2^5 - 2 = 30 usable addresses), can accommodate at least 25 hosts.

From the network given the possible subnets in this range will be:

192.168.10.0/27

192.168.10.32/27

192.168.10.64/27

192.168.10.96/27

The one to be used for this subnet will be **192.168.10.64/27** because 192.168.10.0/27 and 192.168.10.32/27 have been undertaken by the first subnet usable addresses.

The next subnet in this regard must start from 192.168.10.96/27 with the next available CIDR value.

The Finance Department requires up to 10 hosts. We must determine the smallest power of 2 that is higher than or equal to 10 so that we can support 10 hosts.

In this instance, the smallest power of 2 that satisfies the criterion is $2^4(16)$. As a result, 4 bits must be set aside for the host portion of the address.

From the subnet mask given, /24 or 255.255.255.0 as a binary 11111111.11111111.11111111. 00000000 when 4 bits are reserved it will be 11111111.11111111.11111111.11110000 or /28.

We can confidently state that a subnet size of /28, which provides for 16 addresses and $(2^4 - 2 = 14$ usable addresses), can accommodate at least 10 hosts.

From the network given the possible subnets in this range will be:

192.168.10.0/28

192.168.10.16/28

192.168.10.32/28

192.168.10.48/28

192.168.10.64/28

192.168.10.80/28

192.168.10.96/28

192.168.10.112/28

The one to be used for this subnet will be **192.168.10.96/28** because 192.168.10.0/28,192.168.10.16/28,192.168.10.32/28,192.168.10.48/28,1 92.168.10.64/28 and 192.168.10.80/28 has been undertaken by the Marketing and HR subnets as usable addresses.

The next subnet in this regard must start from 192.168.10.112/28 with the next available CIDR value.

The IT department requires up to 6 hosts. We must determine the smallest power of 2 that is higher than or equal to 6 so that we can support 6 hosts.

In this instance, the smallest power of 2 that satisfies the criterion is 2^3(8). As a result, 3 bits must be set aside for the host portion of the address.

From the subnet mask given, /24 or 255.255.255.0 as a binary 11111111.11111111.11111111. 00000000 when 3 bits are reserved it will be 11111111.11111111.11111111.11111000 or /29.

We can confidently state that a subnet size of /29, which provides for 8 addresses (2^3 - 2 = 6 usable addresses), can accommodate at least 6 hosts.

From the network given the possible subnets in this range will be:

192.168.10.0/29

192.168.10.8/29

192.168.10.16/29

192.168.10.24/29

192.18.10.32/29

192.168.10.40/29

192.168.10.48/29

192.168.10.56/29

192.168.10.64/29

192.168.10.72/29

192.168.10.80/29

192.168.10.88/29

192.168.10.96/29

192.168.10.104/29

192.168.10.112/29

192.168.10.120/29

The one to be used for this subnet will be 192.168.10.112/29 because (192.168.10.0/29-192.168.10.104/29) has been undertaken by the Marketing, HR, and Finance subnets as usable addresses.

The next subnet in this regard must start from 192.168.10.120/29 with the next available CIDR value.

Step 3: Determine each subnet's address range.

Marketing Dept Subnet: Range 192.168.10.0 to 192.168.10.63 (62 usable addresses).

HR Dept Subnet: Range 192.168.10.64 to 192.168.10.95 (30 usable addresses).

Finance Dept Subnet: Range 192.168.10.96 to 192.168.10.111 (14 usable addresses).

IT Dept Subnet: Range 192.168.10.112 to 192.168.10.119 (6 usable addresses).

The business may efficiently distribute IP addresses by employing VLSM, making sure that each department gets the right number of addresses based on their requirements. This method improves address use and enhances IP network architecture scalability.

Subnetting is a fundamental strategy for modern network architectures, allowing for smoother operations and faster issue resolution. Subnetting can help with network management and troubleshooting in the following ways:

1. **Reduced Broadcast Traffic**: Broadcast traffic is confined to each subnet in a subnetted network. This decreases the quantity of broadcast traffic that devices must process and aids in the prevention of broadcast storms. As a result, network performance improves and device strain is reduced.

2. **Improved Network Performance**: Because subnetting creates smaller broadcast domains, network resources can be used more efficiently. Devices in a subnet only need to handle broadcast traffic relevant to their subnet, resulting in less needless traffic and improved network performance overall.

3. **Enhanced Security**: Subnetting enables administrators to more effectively deploy security measures. It becomes easier to deploy access restrictions and firewall rules when devices are separated based on their functions or security requirements. Subnetting helps to contain the impact of a security breach inside a particular portion of the network.

4. **Simplified Troubleshooting**: When problems emerge on a subnetted network, network managers can limit the scope

of troubleshooting. They can focus on that portion of the network by isolating a problem to a certain subnet, making it faster to detect and remedy the problem.

5. **Network Segmentation**: Subnetting allows for logical network segmentation. Different departments, offices, or project teams can be established in separate subnets to make managing network traffic and resources easier for each group.

6. **Improved Scalability**: As a network grows, subnetting enables the creation of additional subnets to accommodate the increased number of devices and hosts. This scalability means that the network can grow without generating performance problems or running out of IP address space.

7. **Ease of Network Administration**: Managing a subnetted network is easier than dealing with a flat, non-subnetted network. Administrators can organize devices based on their departments, locations, or functions, making configuration changes, upgrades, and maintenance chores easier to perform.

8. **Simplified Troubleshooting**: When problems emerge on a subnetted network, network managers can limit the scope of troubleshooting. They can focus on that portion of the network by isolating a problem to a certain subnet, making it faster to detect and remedy the problem.

9. **Improved Scalability**: As a network grows, subnetting enables the creation of additional subnets to accommodate the increased number of devices and hosts. This scalability means that the

network can grow without generating performance problems or running out of IP address space.

10. **IP Address Management (IPAM)**: Subnetting improves the efficiency of IP address management. Subnet ranges can be used to assign IP addresses, making it easier to keep track of available and allotted addresses.

3.4.3 Subnetting Examples and Practice

The following real-world examples are intended to provide you with a thorough knowledge of subnetting and to help you cement your learning. By the time you're finished, you'll be confident enough to streamline IP address distribution and clear the way for effective data transfer.

<u>Scenario 1</u>: **Figure out IPv4 Address Subnetting.**

Apply your newfound knowledge to determine the following from the subnet when presented with an IPv4 address, the original subnet mask, and the new subnet mask.

a) Network address
b) Broadcast address
c) Range of host addresses
d) Number of subnets created
e) Number of hosts per subnet

Supplied for IPv4 address	
IP Address of the Host	172.30.54.100
Original Subnet Mask	255.255.0.0
New Subnet Mask:	255.255.240.0
Find	
Number of Subnet Bits	4
Number of Subnets Created	16
Number of Host Bits per Subnet	12
Number of Hosts per Subnet	4094
Network Address of this Subnet	172.30.48.0
IPv4 Address of First Host on this Subnet	172.30.48.1
IPv4 Address of Last Host on this Subnet	172.30.63.254
IPv4 Broadcast Address on this Subnet	172.30.63.255

Analysis

Let's have a look at how this table was put together.

The subnet mask given as original was 255.255.0.0 or /16. The subnet mask given as new is 255.255.240.0 or /20. The difference between the two masks is 4 bits in the third octet when constituted as a binary. We can confidently identify 16 subnets/networks as the result of the 4 bits borrowed ($2^4 = 16$).

The new mask 255.255.240.0 or /20(11111111.11111111.11110000. 00000000) 12 bits are reserved for hosts. With 12 bits left for hosts, we use the following formula: Per subnet, 2^{12}-2 = 4,094 usable hosts/no of hosts per subnet.

To find the subnet for this problem, seek for a number in the 3rd octet (172.30.54.100) that is close to it, exactly it, and not more than it with the least significant bit increment of 16 starting from the smallest network (172.30.0.0). Possible networks with an increment of 16 will be{172.30.0.0,172.30.16.0,172.30.32.0,172.30.48.0,172.30.64.0} In this regard, the network will be **172.30.10.48.0** because 48 in the 3rd octet is closer to 54 and 64 is more than it.

The subnet's broadcast address is the highest address, with all host bits set to 1. Because the host part is only 12 bits long (32 bits - 20 bits subnet mask), the binary representation of the broadcast address will have all host bits set to 1:

Network ID: 10101100.00011110.00110000. 00000000

Broadcast: 10101100.00011110.00111111.11111111

Broadcast Address will therefore be 172.30.63.255 as a decimal. For the 3rd octet, the broadcast address will be the network added to increment less one. In this case 48+16-1=63.For broadcast when the host bits are set to 1 its decimal value will be 255 hence 172.30.63.255.

Finally, for each subnet, you must identify the first, and last addresses within the network and broadcast addresses. Using binary math for the host portion of the address is one approach for determining the host range. The last 12 bits of the address in this regard form the host component. All significant bits on the first host would be set to zero, while the least significant bit would be set to one. All significant bits on the last host would be set to 1 and the least significant bit would be set to

0. The host portion of the address is located in the third and fourth octets in this example.

The first host address will be the network address as it is with the increment of one in the 4th octet (172.30.10.48.1). The last address will be the broadcast address as it is with the decrement of one in the 4th octet (172.30.10.63.254)

Scenario 2:

Determine the following from the subnet when presented with an IPv4 address, the original subnet mask, and the new subnet mask.

1. Network address
2. Broadcast address
3. Range of host addresses
4. Number of subnets created
5. Number of hosts per subnet

Supplied for IPv4 address	
IP Address of the Host	10.0.130.225
Original Subnet Mask	255.0.0.0
New Subnet Mask:	255.255.192.0
Find	
Number of Subnet Bits	10
Number of Subnets Created	1024
Number of Host Bits per Subnet	14
Number of Hosts per Subnet	16382
Network Address of this Subnet	10.0.128.0
IPv4 Address of First Host on this Subnet	10.0.128.1
IPv4 Address of Last Host on this Subnet	10.0.191.254
IPv4 Broadcast Address on this Subnet	10.0.191.255

Analysis

Let's have a look at how this table was put together.

The subnet mask given as original was 255.0.0.0 or /8. The subnet mask given as new is 255.255.192.0 or /18. The difference between the two masks is 10 bits in the third octet when constituted as a binary. We can confidently identify 1024 subnets/networks as the result of the 10 bits borrowed ($2^{10} = 1024$).

The new mask 255.255.192.0 or /18(11111111.11111111.11000000. 00000000) 14 bits are reserved for hosts. With 14 bits left for hosts, we use the following formula: Per subnet, $2^{14} - 2 = 16{,}382$ usable hosts.

To find the subnet for this problem, seek for a number in the 3rd octet (10.0.130.225) that is close to it, exactly it, and not more than it with the least significant bit increment of 64 starting from the smallest network (10.0.0.0). Possible networks with increment of 64 will be {10.0.0.0,10.0.64.0,10.0.128.0,10.0.192.0}.In this regard, the network will be 10.0.128.0 because 128 in the 3rd octet is closer to 130 and 192 is more than it.

The subnet's broadcast address is the highest address, with all host bits set to 1. Because the host part is only 14 bits long (32 bits - 18 bits subnet mask), the binary representation of the broadcast address will have all host bits set to 1:

Network ID: 00001010.00000000.10000000. 00000000

Broadcast: 00001010.00000000.10111111.11111111

Broadcast Address will therefore be 10.0.191.255 as a decimal. For the 3rd octet, the broadcast address will be the network added to increment less one. In this case 128+64-1=191.For broadcast when the host bits are set to 1 its decimal value will be 255 hence 10.0.191.255.

The first host address will be the network address as it is with the increment of one in the 4th octet (10.0.128.1). The last address will be the broadcast address as it is with the decrement of one in the 4th octet (10.0.191.254)

Scenario 3:

Determine the following from the subnet when presented with an IPv4 address, the original subnet mask, and the new subnet mask.

1. Network address
2. Broadcast address
3. Range of host addresses

4. Number of subnets created

5. Number of hosts per subnet

Supplied for IPv4 address	
IP Address of the Host	192.168.10.120
Original Subnet Mask	255.255.255.0
New Subnet Mask:	255.255.255.224
Find	
Number of Subnet Bits	3
Number of Subnets Created	8
Number of Host Bits per Subnet	5
Number of Hosts per Subnet	30
Network Address of this Subnet	192.168.10.96
IPv4 Address of First Host on this Subnet	192.168.10.97
IPv4 Address of Last Host on this Subnet	192.168.10.126
IPv4 Broadcast Address on this Subnet	192.168.10.127

Analysis

Let's have a look at how this table was put together.

The subnet mask given as original was 255.255.255.0 or /24. The subnet mask given as new is 255.255.255.224 or /27. The difference between the two masks is 3 bits in the fourth octet when constituted as a binary. We can confidently identify 8 subnets/networks as the result of the 3 bits borrowed ($2^3 = 8$).

The new mask 255.255.255.224 or

/27(11111111.11111111.11111111.11100000) 5 bits are reserved for hosts. With 5 bits left for hosts, we use the following formula: Per subnet, $2^5 - 2 = 30$ hosts.

To find the subnet for this problem, seek for a number in the 4th octet (192.168.10.120) that is close to it, exactly it, and not more than it with the least significant bit increment of 32 starting from the smallest network (192.168.10.0). Possible networks with an increment of 32 will be{192.168.10.0,192.168.10.32,192.168.10.64,192.168.10.96,192.168.10.1 28}.In this regard, the network will be 192.168.10.96 because 96 in the 4th octet is closer to 120 and 128 is more than it.

The subnet's broadcast address is the highest address, with all host bits set to 1. Because the host part is only 5 bits long (32 bits - 27 bits subnet mask), the binary representation of the broadcast address will have all host bits set to 1:

Network ID: 11000000.10101000.00001010.01100000

Broadcast: 11000000.10101000.00001010.01111111

Broadcast Address will therefore be 192.168.10.127 as a decimal. Alternatively, in the 4th octet, the broadcast address will be the network added to increment less one. In this case 96+32-1=127.

The first host address will be the network address as it is with the increment of one in the 4th octet (192.168.10.97). The last address will be the broadcast address as it is with the decrement of one in the 4th octet (192.168.10.126)

Scenario 4

Let's look at the network requirements for creating a VLSM address scheme using the 192.168.0.128/25 network address and the scenario below.

An upcoming Pharmaceutical firm is set to establish its network as follows:

a) Quality Control Unit

   Need:40 hosts

b) Research and Development Unit

   Need:25 hosts

c) Regulatory Affairs Unit

   Need:5 hosts

d) Production Unit

   Need:4 hosts

e) Microbiology Unit

   Need:4 hosts

f) Warehouse Unit

   Need:2 hosts

Determine the suitability of establishing the network.

We've been assigned a /25 network. Let's look at the available host addresses that can be derived from it.

The host bits from a /25 network will be (11111111.11111111.11111111.10000000)

$2^7 - 2 = 126$

The total number of hosts based on the units given will be $40+25+5+4+4+2 = 80$

We can safely conclude the mask given can accommodate the number of hosts required

Determine Subnet for Quality Control Unit

The IP addresses required for this subnet are 40

We must determine the smallest power of 2 that is higher than 40 so that we can support 40 hosts. In this instance, the smallest power of 2 that satisfies the criterion is $2^6=64$. As a result, 6 bits must be set aside for the host portion of the address. (11111111.11111111.11111111.11000000)

The subnet mask that can support these 40 addresses will be:/26 or 255.255.255.192

The total valid host addresses that will support /26 will be:2^6-2 $= 62$

The network addresses generated by this subnetting will be 192.168.0.128/26 and 192.168.0.192/26

The first network address (**192.168.0.128/26**) will be used for the Quality Control Unit.

Determine Subnet for Research and Development Unit

The IP addresses required for this subnet are 25

We must determine the smallest power of 2 that is higher than 25 so that we can support 25 hosts. In this instance, the smallest power of 2 that satisfies the criterion is $2^5=32$. As a result, 5 bits must be set aside for the host portion of the address. (11111111.11111111.11111111.11100000)

The subnet mask that can support these 25 addresses will be:/27 or 255.255.255.224

The total valid host addresses that will support /27 will be: $2^5 - 2 = 30$

The network addresses generated by this subnetting will be 192.168.0.192/27 and 192.168.0.224/27

The first network address (**192.168.0.192/27**) will be used for the Research and Development Unit.

Determine Subnet for Regulatory Affairs Unit

The IP addresses required for this subnet are 5

We must determine the smallest power of 2 that is higher than 5 so that we can support 5 hosts. In this instance, the smallest power of 2 that satisfies the criterion is $2^3 = 8$. As a result, 3 bits must be set aside for the host portion of the address. (11111111.11111111.11111111.11111000)

The subnet mask that can support these 5 addresses will be:/29 or 255.255.255.248

The total valid host addresses that will support /29 will be: $2^3 - 2 = 6$

The network addresses generated by this subnetting will be 192.168.0.224/29 and 192.168.0.232/29

The first network address (**192.168.0.224/29**) will be used for the Regulatory Affairs Unit

Determine Subnet for Production Unit

The IP addresses required for this subnet are 4

We must determine the smallest power of 2 that is higher than 4 so that we can support 4 hosts. In this instance, the smallest power of 2 that satisfies the criterion is $2^3 = 8$. As a result, 3 bits must be set aside for the host portion of the address. (11111111.11111111.11111111.11111000)

The subnet mask that can support these 5 addresses will be:/29 or 255.255.255.248

The total valid host addresses that will support /29 will be:$2^3-2 = 6$

The network addresses generated by this subnetting will be

192.168.0.232/29 and 192.168.0.240/29

The first network address (**192.168.0.232/29**) will be used for the Production Unit

Determine Subnet for Microbiology Unit

The IP addresses required for this subnet are 4

We must determine the smallest power of 2 that is higher than 4 so that we can support 4 hosts. In this instance, the smallest power of 2 that satisfies the criterion is $2^3=8$. As a result, 3 bits must be set aside for the host portion of the address. (11111111.11111111.11111111.11111000)

The subnet mask that can support these 5 addresses will be:/29 or 255.255.255.248

The total valid host addresses that will support /29 will be:$2^3-2 = 6$

The network addresses generated by this subnetting will be

192.168.0.240/29 and 192.168.0.248/29

The first network address (**192.168.0.240/29**) will be used for Microbiology Unit

Determine Subnet for Warehouse Unit

The IP addresses required for this subnet are 2

We must determine the smallest power of 2 that is higher than 2 so that we can support 2 hosts. In this instance, the smallest power of 2 that satisfies the criterion is $2^2=4$. As a result, 2 bits must be set aside for the host portion of the address. (11111111.11111111.11111111.11111100)

The subnet mask that can support these 2 addresses will be:/30 or 255.255.255.252

Total valid host addresses that will support /30 will be:2^2-2 = 4

The network addresses generated by this subnetting will be

192.168.0.248/30 and 192.168.0.252/30

The first network address (**192.168.0.248/30**) will be used for the Warehouse Unit

3.4.4 Subnetting Guidelines and Best Practices

Network administrators must develop well-organized and efficient subnetting methods that contribute to a reliable and scalable network architecture. The following are various rules and best practices that network administrators should follow to guarantee successful subnetting:

1. **Plan ahead of time:** Plan the network requirements thoroughly before subnetting. Understand the number of devices, hosts, and subnets required, as well as the network's potential future expansion. A well-planned strategy will eliminate the need for regular re-subnetting, which can be disruptive.

2. **Choose the Correct Subnet Mask:** The subnet mask governs the size of the subnet and the number of IP addresses available. It is critical to choose an appropriate subnet mask to support the desired number of hosts while reducing IP waste.

3. **Use Private IP Address Ranges:** To avoid conflicts with public IP addresses on the internet, use private IP address ranges (e.g., 10.0.0.0/8, 172.16.0.0/12, 192.168.0.0/16) for internal networks.

4. **Consider expansion**: When designing subnets, consider future expansion. More IP addresses should be assigned than are now required to allow for new devices and expansion.

5. **Subnet for Function and Location**: Divide the network into sections based on device function or location. To improve network security and performance, divide servers, printers, and user devices into independent subnets.

6. **Avoid Overlapping Subnets:** Make sure that subnets do not overlap, as this might lead to communication problems between devices in separate subnets.

7. **Implement Variable Length Subnet Masking (VLSM):** VLSM provides for the allocation of different subnet masks within the same network, allowing for more efficient use of IP addresses and the ability to accommodate networks of varying sizes.

8. **Use Subnet Zero and Subnet Broadcast Addresses**: While using the first and last subnets for addressing is technically permissible, it is best to avoid doing so to avoid confusion and potential compatibility issues with older network equipment.

9. **Document Subnetting Scheme**: Keep detailed records of the subnetting scheme, including subnet masks, IP address ranges,

and the purpose of each subnet. This documentation will be useful for future reference and troubleshooting.

10. **Consider Security Needs:** By isolating sensitive devices or services, subnetting can improve network security. Create secure subnets and use suitable firewall rules and access controls.

11. **Monitor and Manage Subnets**: Monitor subnet consumption and performance regularly. Consider shifting devices to other subnets if a subnet becomes overcrowded or has performance difficulties.

Review Exercise

1. Given the IPv4 address, the old subnet mask, and the new subnet mask, complete the tables below with the relevant output.

   Challenge 1:

Given	
Address of the host	192.168.0.18
Original subnet mask	255.255.255.0
New subnet mask	255.255.255.240

Find	
Number of Subnet Bits	4
Number of Subnets Created	16
Number of Host Bits per Subnet	4
Number of Hosts per Subnet	14

Network Address of this Subnet	192.168.0.16
Address of First Host on this Subnet	192.168.0.17
Address of Last Host on this Subnet	192.168.0.30
Broadcast Address on this Subnet	192.168.0.31

Let's go through each item step-by-step.

Number of Subnet Bits

✓ Original Subnet Mask: 255.255.255.0

In binary: 11111111.11111111.11111111.00000000

Number of 1s (network bits): 24

✓ New Subnet Mask: 255.255.255.240

In binary: 11111111.11111111.11111111.11110000

Number of 1s (network bits): 28

✓ Number of Subnet Bits:

Subnet bits are the additional bits used for subnetting beyond the original subnet mask.

28 (new subnet mask) - 24 (original subnet mask) = 4 subnet bits

Number of Subnets Created

✓ The number of subnets created is calculated using the formula 2^n where n is the number of subnet bits.

✓ $2^4 = 16$ subnets

Number of Host Bits per Subnet

✓ Total bits in an IPv4 address: 32

✓ Number of network bits (new subnet mask): 28

✓ Number of Host Bits per Subnet:

32 - 28 = 4 host bits

Number of Hosts per Subnet

✓ The number of hosts per subnet is calculated using the formula $2^h - 2$, where h is the number of host bits (subtracting 2 for the network and broadcast addresses).

✓ $2^4 - 2 = 16 - 2 = 14$ hosts per subnet

Network Address of this Subnet

✓ To find the network address, we need to perform a bitwise AND between the IP address and the new subnet mask.

✓ IP Address: 192.168.0.18

In binary: 11000000.10101000.00000000.00010010

✓ New Subnet Mask: 255.255.255.240

In binary: 11111111.11111111.11111111.11110000

✓ Perform a bitwise AND operation:

11000000.10101000.00000000.00010010

11111111.11111111.11111111.11110000

Result: 11000000.10101000.00000000.00010000

✓ Convert the result back to decimal:

Network Address: 192.168.0.16

✓ Address of First Host on this Subnet

The first host address is the network address + 1:

Network Address: 192.168.0.16

First Host Address: 192.168.0.17

✓ Address of Last Host on this Subnet

The last host address is the broadcast address - 1.

First, find the broadcast address.

✓ Broadcast Address on this Subnet

To find the broadcast address, set all host bits to 1 (all bits after the subnet bits).

Network Address: 192.168.0.16

In binary: 11000000.10101000.00000000.00010000

Set the last 4 bits to 1:

11000000.10101000.00000000.00011111

Result: 192.168.0.31

Broadcast Address: 192.168.0.31

✓ Last Host Address

Last Host Address: 192.168.0.31 - 1

192.168.0.30

✓ Using the method shown above on a step-by-step process of how to find:

- Number of Subnet Bits
- Number of Subnets Created
- Number of Host Bits per Subnet
- Number of Hosts per Subnet
- Network Address of this Subnet
- Address of First Host on this Subnet

- Address of Last Host on this Subnet

- Broadcast Address on this Subnet

✓ Undertake Challenge 2, and Challenge 3 to gauge yourself with the answers provided:

Challenge 2:

Given	
Address of the host	172.16.36.250
Original subnet mask	255.255.0.0
New subnet mask	255.255.224.0

Find	
Number of Subnet Bits	3
Number of Subnets Created	8
Number of Host Bits per Subnet	13
Number of Hosts per Subnet	8190
Network Address of this Subnet	172.16.32.0
Address of First Host on this Subnet	172.16.32.1
Address of Last Host on this Subnet	172.16.63.254
Broadcast Address on this Subnet	172.16.63.255

Challenge 3:

Given	
Address of the host	10.130.150.100
Original subnet mask	255.0.0.0

New subnet mask	255.255.128.0

Find	
Number of Subnet Bits	9
Number of Subnets Created	512
Number of Host Bits per Subnet	15
Number of Hosts per Subnet	32766
Network Address of this Subnet	10.130.128.0
Address of First Host on this Subnet	10.130.128.1
Address of Last Host on this Subnet	10.130.254.255
Broadcast Address on this Subnet	10.130.255.255

2. A newly established small medium enterprise, using 192.168.10.0/24 as the network address is shown using the topology below.

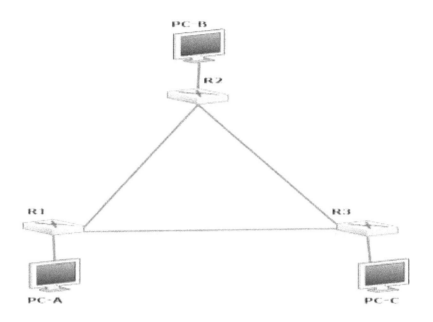

N/B: Every interface of a router forms a network/subnet/broadcast domain.

Required:

a) Ascertain the number of subnets in the network topology

___6___

b) How many bits must you borrow to create the necessary number of subnets? _____3_____

c) What are the usable host addresses per subnet in this addressing scheme? _____30_____

d) In dotted decimal format, what is the new subnet mask?

_255.255.255.224_____

e) How many subnets are accessible for use in the future?

__2____

f) Concerning the subnet information gathered so far, complete the following table

No	Network Address	The first Usable host address	The last usable host address	Broadcast address
0	192.168.1 0.0	192.168.1 0.1	192.168.1 0.30	192.168.1 0.31
1	192.168.1 0.32	192.168.1 0.33	192.168.1 0.62	192.168.1 0.63
2	192.168.1 0.64	192.168.1 0.65	192.168.1 0.94	192.168.1 0.95
3	192.16.10. 96	192.168.1 0.97	192.168.1 0.126	192.168.1 0.127
4	192.168.1 0.128	192.168.1 0.129	192.168.1 0.158	192.168.1 0.159
5	192.168.1 0.160	192.168.1 0.161	192.168.1 0.190	192.168.1 0.191
6	192.168.1 0.192	192.168.1 0.193	192.168.1 0.222	192.168.1 0.223
7	192.168.1 0.224	192.168.1 0.225	192.168.1 0.254	192.168.1 0.255

3. You are provided the network address 192.168.100.0/24 to the subnet and supply the IP address for the network depicted in the topology below.

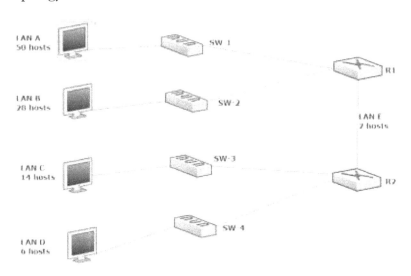

Required:

a) Determine the subnets for the following:

LAN A _192.168.100.0/26

LAN B _192.168.100.64/27

LAN C _192.168.100.96/28

LAN D _192.168.100.112/29

LAN E __192.168.100.120/30

b) Determine the First usable address, last usable address, and broadcast address for the subnets identified in (a)above

Subnet	First Address	Last Address	Broadcast address
LAN-A	192.168.100.1	192.168.100.62	192.168.100.63
LAN-B	192.168.100.65	192.168.100.94	192.168.100.95
LAN-C	192.168.100.97	192.168.100.110	192.18.100.111
LAN-D	192.168.100.113	192.168.100.118	192.168.100.119
LAN-E	192.168.100.121	192.168.100.122	192.168.100.123

Let's go through each item step-by-step.

✓ **Determine the number of host bits needed for each subnet:**

50 hosts: Needs 50 + 2 (network & broadcast) = 52 addresses.

2^6 = 64 addresses, so 6 host bits are needed.

Subnet mask:

32−6=26, so **/26**

28 hosts: Needs 28 + 2 = 30 addresses.

2^5 =32 addresses, so 5 host bits are needed.

Subnet mask:

32−5=27, so **/27**

14 hosts: Needs 14 + 2 = 16 addresses.

2^4 = 16 addresses, so 4 host bits are needed.

Subnet mask:

32−4=28, so **/28**

6 hosts: Needs 6 + 2 = 8 addresses.

2^3 = 8 addresses, so 3 host bits are needed.

Subnet mask:

32−3=29, so **/29**

2 hosts: Needs 2 + 2 = 4 addresses.

2^2 = 4 addresses, so 2 host bits are needed.

Subnet mask:

32−2=30, so **/30**

✓ **Allocate subnets from the 192.168.100.0/24 address space:**

Start from 192.168.100.0 and assign subnets sequentially based on the size calculated above.

Allocation:

Subnet for 50 hosts (/26):

Network address: 192.168.100.0

Subnet mask: 255.255.255.192 (/26)

Address range: 192.168.100.0 - 192.168.100.63

Usable addresses: 192.168.100.1 - 192.168.100.62

Subnet for 28 hosts (/27):

Network address: 192.168.100.64

Subnet mask: 255.255.255.224 (/27)

Address range: 192.168.100.64 - 192.168.100.95

Usable addresses: 192.168.100.65 - 192.168.100.94

Subnet for 14 hosts (/28):

Network address: 192.168.100.96

Subnet mask: 255.255.255.240 (/28)

Address range: 192.168.100.96 - 192.168.100.111

Usable addresses: 192.168.100.97 - 192.168.100.110

Subnet for 6 hosts (/29):

Network address: 192.168.100.112

Subnet mask: 255.255.255.248 (/29)

Address range: 192.168.100.112 - 192.168.100.119

Usable addresses: 192.168.100.113 - 192.168.100.118

Subnet for 2 hosts (/30):

Network address: 192.168.100.120

Subnet mask: 255.255.255.252 (/30)

Address range: 192.168.100.120 - 192.168.100.123

Usable addresses: 192.168.100.121 - 192.168.100.122

By following these steps, we have effectively subnetted the 192.168.100.0/24 network to accommodate the specified number of hosts in each subnet, ensuring efficient utilization of the available IP address space

Chapter 4: IPv4 Address Assignment

IPv4 address assignment describes the process of allocating unique numerical IDs to devices connected to an Internet Protocol version 4 (IPv4) network. Each device, whether a computer, smartphone, printer, or server, must have a unique 32-bit address in the IPv4 addressing scheme to enable seamless communication across the internet's interconnected web of networks. This can happen either dynamically when a server allocates addresses on the fly using DHCP, or statically, where addresses are manually defined. Understanding the concepts of IPv4 address assignment is critical for network design, management, and troubleshooting since it serves as the foundation upon which data packets are routed, enabling the efficient flow of information throughout the global digital landscape.

4.1 Manual Configuration (Static IP)

A static IP address assignment is a method of configuring a network device with a constant and unchanging Internet Protocol (IP) address. Static IP addresses are those that are manually allocated to a device, such as a computer, router, server, or printer, and remain constant over time, even after reboots or network modifications.

Here's a step-by-step guide to assigning static IP addresses:

1. **Identify the Device:** Determine which network devices require a static IP address. It could be any network-capable equipment, such as a computer, printer, router, or server.

2. **Examine the Network Range**: Determine your network's IP address range. This is usually in the form of a subnet, which is indicated by the subnet mask. A common subnet mask, such as 255.255.255.0, indicates that the first three octets represent the network component, while the final octet is allocated for host addresses.

3. **Select an IP Address**: Choose an IP address that is inside your network's IP address range. Make sure the address you've chosen isn't already in use by another device. To avoid conflicts, keep a list of used IP addresses.

4. **Access Network Settings**: To configure the static IP address, go to the network settings of the device you wish to give it to. The procedures for accessing network settings may differ based on the type of device (e.g., computer, router, printer).

4.2 Dynamic Host Configuration Protocol (DHCP)

Network devices are given IP addresses and other network configuration options automatically using the Dynamic Host Configuration Protocol (DHCP). It makes maintaining IP addresses and network settings easier, especially in big networks where manual configuration would be impracticable and error-prone. DHCP works on a client-server basis, with a DHCP server dynamically assigning IP addresses to DHCP clients.

An IPv4 address is assigned, or leased, by the DHCPv4 server from a pool of addresses for a certain period or until the client no longer needs the address. Clients lease information from the server for a predetermined amount of time. Administrators set up DHCPv4 servers to time out leases at varied intervals. The leasing period can range from 24 hours to a week or more. When the lease ends, the client must request a new address.

DHCPv4 Service Operation

1. The client uses the leased IPv4 address to connect to the network until the lease expires. To prolong the lease, the client must contact the DHCP server regularly.

2. This lease method ensures that clients who turn off their power do not keep addresses they no longer use.

3. The DHCP server returns the address to the pool after a lease expires so that it can be reallocated as necessary.

Steps to Secure a Lease

When a client boots (or otherwise wishes to join a network), the following process to secure a lease begins.

Let's look at the following two scenarios:

Scenario 1: Home Network

Consider a scenario in which many devices, such as laptops, smartphones, and smart TVs, are connected to a Wi-Fi router, which serves as the DHCP server.

1. The moment a device (DHCP client) connects to the network or requests an IP address renewal (typically after a lease expires), it broadcasts a **DHCP Discover** message.

2. The broadcast message is received by the DHCP server, which is the Wi-Fi router, and it is responded to with a **DHCP Offer**. The offer includes a free IP address as well as network configuration

details such as the subnet mask, default gateway, and DNS server addresses.

3. If more than one DHCP server is present on the network, the client receives numerous DHCP Offers and chooses one based on the information provided in the offers.

4. When the client chooses the preferred offer, it sends a **DHCP Request** to the selected DHCP server, signifying acceptance of the supplied configuration.

5. The DHCP server then responds with a **DHCP Acknowledgement** (DHCP ACK) message. This notification confirms that the client's IP address, as well as the other network settings, have been assigned.

6. The client now configures its network interface with the parameters obtained, enabling it to communicate on the network using the supplied IP address.

Scenario 2: Corporate Network

Consider a huge corporate network that has hundreds of devices such as computers, printers, and IP phones. In this case, a dedicated DHCP server (usually a server machine or a network appliance) is used to manage IP address assignments.

1. When a new device connects to a network, it broadcasts a **DHCP Discover** message.

2. In this case, the broadcast is received by the DHCP server, which then sends back a DHCP Offer with an IP address from the network segment's designated address pool.

3. After receiving the offer, the client sends a **DHCP Request** expressing its acceptance.

4. With a **DHCP ACK**, the DHCP server acknowledges the request, and the client now has a valid IP address as well as other setup parameters.

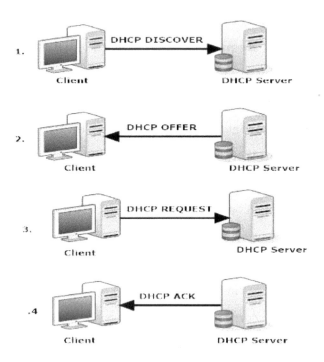

Steps to renew a Lease

Before the lease expires, the client starts a two-step process with the DHCPv4 server to renew the lease.

5. Request for **DHCP (DHCPREQUEST)**

Before the lease expires, the client sends a DHCPREQUEST message to the original DHCPv4 server that provided the

IPv4 address. If a DHCPACK is not received within a certain length of time, the client broadcasts another DHCP REQUEST for one of the other DHCPv4 servers to extend the lease.

6. **DHCPACK** (DHCP Acknowledgement)

When the server receives the DHCPREQUEST message, it checks the lease information by returning a DHCPACK.

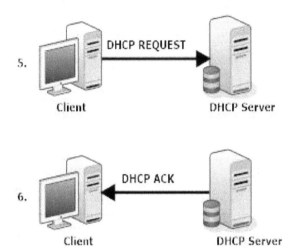

DHCPv4 Configuration

The following configuration commands can be found in a router or DHCP server. Please keep in mind that the particular configuration may differ depending on the device's vendor and type, as well as the requirements of the network. This example assumes a simple network configuration.

Description	Command
Configuration of IP address on the router's interface that will act as the default gateway.	Router(config)#interface GigabitEthernet0/0 ip address 192.168.0.1 255.255.255.0
Configure address to be excluded from being assigned to Clients	Router(config)#ip dhcp excluded-address 192.168.0.1
Configure the DHCP pool with its parameters as follows:	
Configuration of DHCP pool	Router(config)#ip dhcp pool LAN_A
The network address and subnet mask for the pool	Router(dhcp-config)# network 192.168.0.0 255.255.255.0
Default gateway for clients	Router(dhcp-config)#default-router 192.168.0.1
DNS server IP Address {Illustrative example the google server}	Router(dhcp-config) #dns-server 8.8.4.4
Domain name for the network	Router(dhcp-config)#domain-name xyz.com
Lease time for the IP address (Example given:2days 12hrs and 30mins).	Router(dhcp-config) #lease 2 12 30

Save your work to Non-Volatile Random-access memory (NVRAM)	Router(dhcp-config) #do write

Advantages of DHCP:

1. Simplified Network Administration: DHCP eliminates the requirement for each device to manually configure its IP address, saving time and lowering the risk of human mistakes.
2. Effective IP Address Utilization: DHCP ensures that IP addresses are assigned dynamically and released when no longer needed, resulting in more effective use of available IP address space.
3. DHCP facilitates centralized management and setting of IP addresses in bigger networks, making it easier to monitor and control network devices.
4. Device Integration Simplified: When new devices are introduced to the network, they can immediately receive the necessary network settings via DHCP, allowing for smooth integration.

4.3 Automatic Private IP Addressing (APIPA)

Automatic Private IP Addressing (APIPA) is a function in certain operating systems, such as Windows, that allows a device to be automatically assigned an IP address when it cannot receive one from a DHCP server. The device is given a private IP address by APIPA from a predetermined range, enabling communication with other devices connected to the same local network segment. On the other hand, devices with IP addresses allocated by APIPA are unable to communicate with other devices outside of their local network.

When a device connects to a network, it normally requires an IP address, which serves as its network identification. This IP address allows the gadget to communicate with other devices and connect to the internet. When devices connect to a network, a special server known as a DHCP server assigns them IP addresses automatically. However, the DHCP server may be busy, malfunctioning, or unavailable on the network at times. In such instances, if the device is unable to obtain its usual IP address, APIPA will be supplied.

With APIPA, the device assigns itself a temporary IP address from a particular range specified for this purpose. The APIPA range is a specific range of IP addresses that begins with "**169.254.**"

Here are several situations in which Automatic Private IP Addressing (APIPA) might be used:

DHCP Server Unavailable

Scenario: A network to a computer or device with a DHCP server, but the DHCP server is now offline or not responding for any reason.

In an office network, for example, a user brings their laptop into a meeting room and connects to the local network. However, due to a brief DHCP server failure, the laptop is unable to receive an IP address. In this instance, APIPA takes effect, and the laptop allocates itself an IP address from the APIPA range.

APIPA addresses range from **169.254.0.1** to **169.254.255.254**.

Misconfigured Network or Cable Disconnection

Scenario: A network cable is unplugged from a device, or the network settings are misconfigured, preventing the device from getting a valid IP address. For example, suppose a computer is linked to a router, but the network cable was unintentionally unplugged or there is a problem with the cable itself. The computer's connection to the DHCP server is lost as a result, and APIPA assigns it an automatic private IP address so that it can keep in touch with other devices on the local network.

Ad-Hoc Network Setup

APIPA might be beneficial in ad-hoc network settings, where devices form a network among themselves without a dedicated DHCP server, to enable communication.

For example, a group of coworkers brings their laptops to a conference room to work on a project. They establish an ad hoc network by wirelessly linking their devices. Because this ad-hoc network lacks a DHCP server, APIPA is used to automatically assign IP addresses to each laptop, allowing them to converse and share files within the ad-hoc network.

DHCP Server Misconfiguration

The DHCP server is present on the network, but it is incorrectly configured, resulting in failed IP address assignments.

In a small office network, for example, the DHCP server is configured to manage IP address assignments. A recent configuration update or a software issue, on the other hand, causes the DHCP server to fail. Devices that connect to the network during this period will not be assigned IP addresses, and APIPA will be triggered to assign them automatic private IP addresses for local communication.

It is crucial to remember that, while APIPA can be useful in some instances, it is not a replacement for good DHCP management. Devices using APIPA addresses should switch back to getting legitimate IP addresses from the DHCP server whenever the DHCP server becomes available or the underlying network difficulties are fixed.

Review Exercise

1. Using the topology below, Configure the router to act as a DHCP Server and Assign Client Computer IP addresses automatically based on the network addresses given.

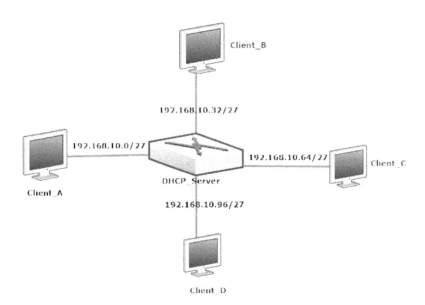

Additional information

LAN-A:192.168.10.0/27

LAN-B:192.168.10.32/27

LAN-C:192.168.10.64/27

LAN-D:192.168.10.96/27

For this illustration we shall use Packet tracer as a simulation software: The configuration that makes the router a DHCP server is as follows:

```
Step 1:First Usable IP Address configuration for each network on the Router
DHCP_Server(config)#int f0/1
DHCP_Server(config-if)#ip address 192.168.10.1 255.255.255.224
DHCP_Server(config-if)#no shutdown

DHCP_Server(config-if)#int f0/0
DHCP_Server(config-if)#ip address 192.168.10.33 255.255.255.224
DHCP_Server(config-if)#no shutdown

DHCP_Server(config-if)#int f1/1
DHCP_Server(config-if)#ip address 192.168.10.65 255.255.255.224
DHCP_Server(config-if)#no shutdown

DHCP_Server(config-if)#int f1/0
DHCP_Server(config-if)#ip address 192.168.10.97 255.255.255.224
DHCP_Server(config-if)#no shutdown
DHCP_Server(config-if)#end
DHCP_Server#write
Building configuration...
[OK]
```

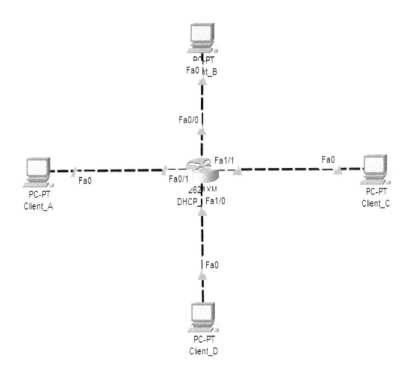

Step 2:Configuring the Router as DHCP Server
DHCP_Server(config)#ip dhcp excluded-address 192.168.10.1
DHCP_Server(config)#ip dhcp pool LAN-A
DHCP_Server(dhcp-config)#network 192.168.10.0 255.255.255.224
DHCP_Server(dhcp-config)#default-router 192.168.10.1
DHCP_Server(dhcp-config)#dns-server 8.8.4.4

DHCP_Server(config)#ip dhcp excluded-address 192.168.10.33
DHCP_Server(config)#ip dhcp pool LAN-B
DHCP_Server(dhcp-config)#network 192.168.10.32 255.255.255.224
DHCP_Server(dhcp-config)#default-router 192.168.10.33
DHCP_Server(dhcp-config)#dns-server 8.8.4.4

DHCP_Server(dhcp-config)#ip dhcp excluded-address 192.168.10.65
DHCP_Server(config)#ip dhcp pool LAN-C
DHCP_Server(dhcp-config)#network 192.168.10.64 255.255.255.224
DHCP_Server(dhcp-config)#default-router 192.168.10.65
DHCP_Server(dhcp-config)#dns-server 8.8.4.4

DHCP_Server(dhcp-config)#ip dhcp excluded-address 192.168.10.97
DHCP_Server(config)#ip dhcp pool LAN-D
DHCP_Server(dhcp-config)#network 192.168.10.96 255.255.255.224
DHCP_Server(dhcp-config)#default-router 192.168.10.97
DHCP_Server(dhcp-config)#dns-server 8.8.4.4
DHCP_Server(dhcp-config)#end
DHCP_Server#write
Building configuration...
[OK]

Confirmation of the IP address from Client_A PC

2. Why is the DHCPREQUEST message issued as a broadcast when a client requests an initial address lease from a DHCP server?

   A. The broadcast serves to implicitly reject any other offers the client may have gotten from other servers if there were any.

   B. The DHCP server that issued the offer's IP address was not yet known by the client.

   C. The client cannot transmit a unicast message at layer 2 since it has not yet been issued a MAC address.

   D. A broadcast request must be sent because the DHCP server can be on a different subnet.

Explanation

When a client first asks for an IP address lease from a DHCP server, it sends out a DHCPREQUEST message as a broadcast for a variety of reasons, the most common of which is that the client may not know which DHCP server provided the IP address. This is significant because the DHCPREQUEST message is a request to the server that provided the IP address, and broadcasting ensures that the message reaches all available DHCP servers on the network, including the one that made the offer.

3. The information below is contained in which DHCP IPv4 message?

     ✓ Destination address: 255.255.255.255

     ✓ Subnet mask: 0.0.0.0

     ✓ IPv4 address: 0.0.0.0

     ✓ Default gateway address: 0.0.0.0

A. <u>DHCP DISCOVER</u>

B. DHCP REQUEST

C. DHCP OFFER

D. DHCP ACK

Explanation

Destination address: 255.255.255.255: This indicates that the message is broadcast, which is typical for the initial DHCPDISCOVER message since the client does not yet know the address of the DHCP server.

Subnet mask: 0.0.0.0: This shows that the client is not aware of the network configuration.

IPv4 address: 0.0.0.0: The client has not been assigned an IP address yet, which is why it's using 0.0.0.0.

Default gateway address: 0.0.0.0: The client also doesn't know the gateway at this point.

During the DHCP process, a client starts by broadcasting a DHCPDISCOVER message to find available DHCP servers on the network. This message typically contains the values listed above, indicating that the client currently has no IP configuration.

Chapter 5: Address Resolution Protocol (ARP)

The Address Resolution Protocol (ARP) is a protocol that dynamically maps an IP (Internet Protocol) address to a corresponding MAC (Media Access Control) address. It operates at the OSI (Open Systems Interconnection) model's data link layer (Layer 2), which is responsible for the reliable transmission of data between devices on the same local network. When only IP addresses are known, ARP allows devices to discover each other's physical hardware addresses.

The following are the primary goals of ARP:

1. **IP-to-MAC Address Mapping:** One of the key responsibilities of ARP is to determine the MAC address associated with a certain IP address on the same local network. IP addresses are used for logical addressing, allowing devices to identify each other within a network, whereas MAC addresses are used for physical addressing, identifying devices on a local network based on their unique hardware identifiers. ARP supports the mapping of these two sorts of addresses, allowing proper data transport between devices.

   Example

   If a device, such as a computer with the source IP address 172.16.10.10, wishes to interact with another device on the same local network, such as 172.16.10.20, it must know the destination device's MAC address. The computer will issue an ARP request, inquiring, "Who has IP address 172.16.10.20?" The computer will update its ARP cache with this mapping after the device with the IP address 172.16.10.20 responds with its MAC address. Subsequent data packets bound for 172.16.10.20 will utilize the correct MAC address, ensuring that communication is successful.

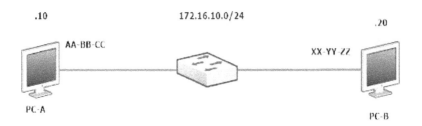

Destination Mac	Source Mac	Source IPv4	Destination IPv4
XX-YY-ZZ	AA-BB-CC	172.16.10.10	172.16.10.20

Summary

PC-A wishes to transmit a packet to PCB in this scenario. The diagram shows the Layer 2 source and destination MAC addresses as well as the Layer 3 IPv4 addressing that would be present in the packet that PC-A would send.

The following is included in the Layer 2 Ethernet frame:

Destination MAC address – The PC-B's MAC address is XX-YY-ZZ from the example given.

Source MAC address – The Ethernet NIC on PC-A's MAC address is AA-BB-CC From the example given.

The following is included in the Layer 3 IP packet:

Source IPv4 address – PC-A's IPv4 address is 172.16.10.10.

Destination IPv4 address – PC-B's IPv4 address is 172.16.10.20.

2. **Packet Forwarding on a Local Network:** When a device wishes to send data to another device on the same local network, it must first discover the destination device's MAC address based on its IP address. ARP enables devices to conduct this mapping, guaranteeing that data packets reach their appropriate target. ARP plays an important role in packet forwarding inside a local network by resolving IP addresses to MAC addresses.

Example

Consider a scenario where a smartphone connected to a Wi-Fi network wishes to visit a website hosted on a server with the IP address 192.168.0.150. The smartphone must first determine the server's MAC address. It issues an ARP request, to which the server answers with its MAC address. This MAC address is then used by the smartphone to send data packets to the server, providing for a seamless connection.

3. **Address Caching and Efficiency:** Most operating systems and networking equipment utilize ARP and keep an ARP cache or table. The ARP cache maintains IP-to-MAC address mappings that have recently been resolved. ARP can circumvent the

resolution procedure when a device has to communicate with another device whose IP-to-MAC mapping is already in the cache, resulting in faster and more efficient data

Example

A user's laptop regularly talks with the home router in a home network. When the laptop determines the router's MAC address via ARP, it keeps this mapping in its ARP cache. The laptop utilizes the cached MAC address the next time it has to send data to the router, bypassing the requirement for ARP resolution and speeding up the communication process.

4. **Host Configuration and Initialization:** A network-enabled device may use ARP during the boot process to announce its presence and collect the necessary IP-to-MAC mappings to ensure proper network connection. This is especially significant in DHCP (Dynamic Host Configuration Protocol) setups where devices must receive IP addresses regularly.

Example

When a new device connects to a network with DHCP enabled, it must get an IP address and other setup settings. The device communicates with the DHCP server over ARP to seek an IP address. ARP supports this initial communication, allowing the device to configure itself and join the network.

5.1 ARP Broadcast and Unicast

ARP communicates through two unique methods: broadcast and unicast. Broadcast ARP is used to discover the MAC address of a specific IP address throughout the entire network, whereas Unicast ARP is used to resolve addresses between two devices. Understanding the complexities of ARP's broadcast and unicast behaviors is critical for understanding the underlying mechanics that drive efficient and dependable network communication.

Using appropriate examples, let's look at two instances in which ARP messages are broadcast and when they are unicast:

Illustration: Broadcast Message

Consider the following scenario: Device X wishes to interact with another device, Device Y, on the same local area network (LAN). However, Device X only knows Device Y's IP address and must discover its MAC address to establish a direct connection.

1. In this case, Device X broadcasts an ARP broadcast message (ARP request) to the entire network, asking, "Who possesses IP address A.A.A.A? Please provide me with your MAC address." This broadcast message is received by all devices on the LAN.

2. Unicast ARP Reply: After receiving the ARP request and detecting that the IP address matches its own, Device Y sends a unicast ARP reply directly to Device X. The reply includes its MAC address, so Device X now has the information it needs to communicate with Device Y.

Illustration: Unicast Message

Consider the following scenario: A device, Device A, has recently joined the LAN and wishes to update its ARP cache with the MAC-to-IP mapping of another device, Device B.

Unicast ARP Update: Device A, without knowing Device B's MAC address, sends a unicast ARP request directly to Device B, asking, "What is your MAC address?" "I need to update my ARP cache." This communication is sent only to Device B.

Unicast Gratuitous ARP: Let's Assume Device B wants to proactively update the ARP caches of all other devices on the network with its current MAC-to-IP mapping (e.g., in the event of a network configuration change or for redundancy considerations). In such a situation, it can broadcast a unicast gratuitous ARP response to each device, updating their ARP caches individually with the updated information.

5.2 ARP Caching and ARP Table

The ARP table, also known as the ARP cache, is a fundamental data structure used to store and manage resolved IP-to-MAC address mappings. Its main job is to maintain a local area network's (LAN) record of the associations between IP addresses and their corresponding MAC addresses. To avoid making repeated ARP resolution requests and improve network speed, a device that needs to interact with another device on the same network looks in the ARP table to find the MAC address associated with the target IP address.

The ARP table and its purpose in storing resolved IP-to-MAC mappings are described below:

1. **ARP Request and Reply Process**

   When a network device (for example, Device X) wants to interact with another network device (for example, Device Y) whose IP address it knows but not the matching MAC address, it sends an

ARP request. The ARP request is broadcast to all devices on the LAN.

Device Y answers with an ARP reply, transmitting its MAC address back to Device X through a unicast message.

2. **Storing IP-to-MAC Mappings**

When Device X receives an ARP response from Device Y, it adds the IP-to-MAC mapping to its ARP table.

3. **ARP Cache Timeout and Aging**

The ARP cache timeout limits the lifetime of ARP cache entries. This timeout is usually only a few minutes long. The ARP item remains valid and is not removed from the table as long as Device X interacts with Device Y within the timeout interval.

If Device X does not interact with Device Y for an extended or specified time, the entry may age out and be removed from the ARP table. This adaptive aging ensures that the ARP table contains only relevant mappings.

4. **ARP Table Lookup**

When Device X needs to interact with Device Y again, it first consults the ARP database to determine the IP-to-MAC mapping. If the mapping is still intact and valid (has not expired), Device X can use the MAC address from the ARP table to deliver unicast packets directly to Device Y without the requirement for ARP broadcast and resolution.

5. **Network Efficiency Optimization**

   The ARP table increases network efficiency and minimizes ARP traffic by storing resolved IP-to-MAC mappings. Because devices can quickly get MAC addresses from the ARP table, frequent ARP broadcasts are reduced, enhancing network responsiveness and lowering latency.

5.3 ARP Network Segmentation

ARP is used to determine the MAC address of the destination device when two devices connect within the same network segment. However, when devices need to connect across network segments, such as in a routed network, ARP behaves differently.

Let's go over the way ARP works in different network segments:

1. **Same Network Segment (Local Communication)**

   Devices in a local network segment are linked to the same physical network and share the same IP subnet. When a device wishes to interact with another device on the same network, it first checks its ARP cache to verify if it already has the destination device's MAC address. If the MAC address is not detected in the cache, the device broadcasts an ARP broadcast message (ARP request) to the entire local network and asks, "Who has IP address X?" The device with the matching IP address responds with its MAC address (ARP reply), and the asking device stores this information in its ARP cache. Subsequent communications between the two devices can then take place directly utilizing their MAC addresses.

2. **Different Network Segments (Remote Communication)**

ARP behaves differently when devices need to connect across network segments, such as in a routed network. Because they are not on the same local network, devices in different network segments cannot communicate directly using MAC addresses. Instead, the following happens:

a) **ARP Resolution in the Local Segment**

Consider the case where a device on Network A wishes to communicate with a device on Network B. The source device must first resolve the MAC address of the default gateway (router) that connects Network A to Network B before it may deliver data. It goes through the same ARP procedure as before, but this time it looks for the MAC address of the router's interface that is in the same network segment as the source device

b) **Packet Routing to the Destination Network**

Once the source device knows the MAC address of the router's interface (in the same network segment), it encapsulates the data in a packet that includes the destination IP address (from Network B) and the MAC address of the router's interface. The packet is then sent to the router by the source device.

c) **Router ARP Resolution**

The packet is received by the router from the source device. It looks at the destination IP address to see which of its interfaces is connected to Network B. Before it can forward the packet, the router must first resolve the MAC address of the target device (on Network B). The router employs the same ARP procedure, broadcasting an ARP request on Network B to get the MAC address of the destination device.

d) **Sending the Packet to the Destination Device**

When the router learns the destination device's MAC address, it modifies the packet's destination MAC address and passes it to the destination device on Network B.

ARP facilitates communication between devices across multiple network segments in a routed network by doing these steps. It assists devices in determining the correct MAC address of routers and other devices on their local network segment, allowing for proper data routing between networks.

Review Exercise

1. What would be contained in a frame transmitted from a source device to a destination device on the same local network in terms of the destination MAC address?

   A. The device broadcast the physical address of FF-FF-FF-FF-FF-FF

   B. The destination device's mac address

   C. The router's local interface's Mac address

   D. Mac address of remote subnet interface

   Explanation

When a source device sends a frame to another device on the same local network, the frame includes the destination device's MAC address.

2. Which of the following protocols is employed to ascertain the MAC address of a known destination device's Internet Protocol (IP) address?

A. DHCP

B. DNS

C. ARP

D. HTTP

Explanation

ARP is specifically designed to map IP addresses to MAC addresses within a local network, enabling devices to communicate at the data link layer.

Chapter 6: Network Address Translation (NAT)

The world lives on connectivity in the wide expanse of the digital sphere, with billions of gadgets communicating over the internet. The Internet Protocol (IP) and its IPv4 addressing system, which has been the Internet's backbone for decades, is at the heart of this seamless communication. However, as the online landscape has rapidly expanded and there has been an extraordinary spike in the number of internet-connected devices, the supply of unique IPv4 addresses has reduced, posing a serious barrier to the digital ecosystem's long-term growth.

Network Address Translation (NAT) is a groundbreaking technology that has become an essential component of modern networking. NAT is critical in alleviating the scarcity of IPv4 addresses by allowing numerous devices within a private network to share a single, globally routable public IP address. This innovative solution assures that devices with private IP addresses can communicate with external networks, including the global internet while conserving valuable IPv4 addresses.

The IPv4 address space was thought to be enormous at its introduction, with around 4.3 billion distinct addresses available. The number of internet-capable devices, from PCs and smartphones to Internet of Things (IoT) devices, has surpassed the number of IPv4 addresses that are currently available.

Network Address Translation allows a local network, such as a home or business network, to use private IP addresses that are not directly reachable from the public internet. When data is transferred from a private network to the internet, NAT functions as an intermediary, transforming the source private IP addresses to a single public IP address accessible to the outside world. As data packets return from the internet, NAT performs reverse translation, sending the data to the appropriate device within the private network.

We will look at many types of NAT, such as static NAT, dynamic NAT, and port address translation (PAT). It is now time to unravel the complexity of Network Address Translation and see how this innovative approach overcomes the IPv4 address gap, allowing our interconnected digital society to continue to flourish and prosper. Understanding NAT is critical for understanding the backbone of modern internet communication, whether you are a networking enthusiast, a student, or an IT professional. Let's go on this expedition and explore the world of Network Address Translation.

6.1 Types of NAT

Static NAT

Static NAT entails translating a private IP address to a corresponding public IP address on a one-to-one basis. This sort of NAT is commonly employed when an internal device within a private network requires a consistent, publicly available identity. It ensures that the internal device uses the same public IP address for both outgoing and inbound communications, making it suitable for servers or devices that require persistent internet access.

Static NAT entails translating a private IP address to a corresponding public IP address on a one-to-one basis. This sort of NAT is commonly employed when an internal device within a private network requires a consistent, publicly available identity. It ensures that the internal device uses the same public IP address for both outgoing and inbound communications, making it suitable for servers or devices that require persistent internet access.

Example:

Assume a corporation has a web server with a private IP address of 10.0.0.10 on its internal network. To make the web server visible to internet users, the IT administrator configures a static NAT rule that maps a private IP address (10.0.0.10) to a public IP address (197.0.116.6). When external users browse the company's website, their requests are directed to the public IP address (197.0.116.6), and the static NAT guarantees that these requests are forwarded to the web server with the private IP address (10.0.0.10).

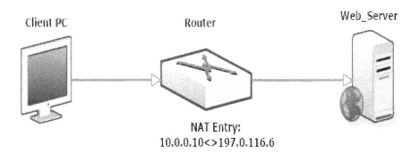

Sample illustration of static NAT implementation.

Dynamic NAT

In contrast to static NAT, dynamic NAT employs a pool of public IP addresses that are dynamically assigned to internal devices. NAT dynamically picks an accessible public IP address from the pool and maps it to the internal device's private IP address whenever an internal device makes an outbound connection. Multiple devices within the private network can thus share a limited number of public IP addresses.

Example:

Consider the following scenario: a small office with 10 PCs (devices) connected to the internet via a router. Dynamic NAT is enabled on the router, with a pool of five public IP addresses (197.0.116.6 - 197.0.116.10). When Computer X seeks access to a website, the NAT provides it with the pool's first public IP address 197.0.116.6. When Computer Y makes a connection, it receives the pool's next available public IP address, such as 197.0.116.7. As a result, all 10 PCs in the business can share a restricted pool of public IP addresses for internet communications as needed.

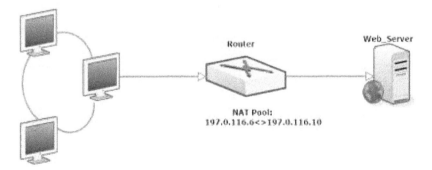

Sample illustration of Dynamic NAT implementation

Port Address Translation (PAT)

Port address translation, also known as Network Address Port Translation (NAPT), expands on the notion of Dynamic NAT by employing unique port numbers in addition to public IP addresses to differentiate between internal devices. Because the public IP address and port number are combined, many internal devices can use the same public IP address at the same time.

When the NAT router receives a packet from a client using PAT, the source port number is used to uniquely identify the individual NAT translation.

PAT ensures that devices use a unique TCP port number for each connection with an internet server.

Example

Consider a home network with many devices (for example, cell phones, laptops, and game consoles) linked to the Internet via a single public IP address issued by the Internet Service Provider (ISP). PAT is enabled on the router in the home network. When Device X visits a website, the router assigns it a public IP address, such as 197.0.116.6, as well as a unique source port number (for example, 520). When Device Y accesses a different website, it is assigned the same public IP address (197.0.116.6) but with a different source port number (e.g.,1024). The router records these port allocations, allowing several devices to effectively share the same public IP address.

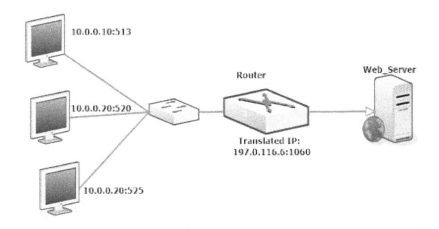

Sample illustration of Port address translation implementation

In conclusion, Static NAT, Dynamic NAT, and PAT are essential methods for managing the restricted pool of public IPv4 addresses. Each type has distinct advantages and is appropriate for a variety of scenarios, ranging from providing consistent access to specified servers (Static NAT) to allowing several devices to share a limited number of public IP addresses (Dynamic NAT and PAT). Understanding different NAT types is essential for networking experts who want to improve their network infrastructure.

6.2 How NAT works

We've already discussed the way Network Address Translation (NAT) allows devices on a local network with private IP addresses to communicate with devices on the internet that use public IP addresses. By hiding private IP addresses from the public internet, it also aids in the conservation of IPv4 address space and increases security for internal networks.

Let's investigate how NAT works:

1. **Private and Public IP Addresses**

   NAT uses two kinds of IP addresses: private and public. Private IP addresses are allocated for usage within a local network and are not routable on the public internet. Public IP addresses, on the other hand, are globally unique and routable over the internet.

2. **Local Network Setup**

   Computers, smartphones, printers, and other devices are common components of a local network. These devices are issued private IP addresses from a predefined range, such as those described in RFC 1918 (for example, 192.168.0.0/16, 172.16.0.0/12, or 10.0.0.0/8).

3. **NAT Router**

   A NAT router is an internetworking device that connects the local network to the internet (typically in conjunction with a firewall). The router contains at least two network interfaces, one for the local network (LAN) and the other for internet access (WAN).

4. **Outbound Traffic (Local to Internet)**

   An outbound connection is initiated when a device on the local network wishes to interact with a server on the internet. The device sends a packet to the NAT router with a source IP address (private IP) and a source port number. When the packet arrives at the NAT router, it substitutes the source IP address with the NAT router's public IP address (which it acquired from the internet service provider). The router also alters the source port number, which aids in translation tracking. The updated packet is subsequently sent to the internet's destination server.

5. **Inbound Traffic (Internet to Local)**

   When a server on the internet responds to the device's request, the response packet is sent to the public IP address of the NAT router. The NAT router evaluates the incoming packet's destination IP address and port number. The router recognizes the internal device that issued the initial request and transmits the packet to it using its translation table (which maintains track of the mappings). The router converts the destination IP address to the internal device's private IP address and restores the source port number. The packet is subsequently transmitted to the relevant local network device.

6. **Translation Table**

   The NAT router keeps a translation table that records the mappings between private IP addresses, private port numbers, public IP addresses, and public port numbers. This table helps the router to keep track of current connections and execute address translations for incoming and outgoing packets.

6.3 NAT Configuration on a Cisco Router

Static NAT

The following steps are necessary to configure Static NAT on a Cisco router:

1. Use the ip nat inside command to configure the router's internal interface.

2. Use the ip nat outside command to configure the router's external interface.

3. Configure static NAT mapping for the internal server/host you want to expose to the internet.

Description	Command
Define the Router's internal interface	Router(config)#interface g0/0
Configure NAT inside a command to the router's internal interface	Router(config-if)#ip nat INSIDE
Define the Router's external interface	Router(config-if)#interface se0/3/0
Configure NAT outside command to the router's interface	Router(config-if)#ip nat OUTSIDE

Configure static NAT mapping for the internal server/host	Router(config)#ip nat inside source static 10.0.0.10 197.0.116.6

After configuring static NAT, you must be able to validate the setup. We can use the following commands to validate the NAT translations:

Description	Command
To view basic IP address translation information	Router#show ip nat translation
To clear dynamic translation	Router# clear ip nat translation *
To view information about the total number of active translations	Router#show ip nat statistics
To clear statistics from any past translations	Router#clear ip nat statistics
To view NAT operation and display information about each packet the router translates	Router#debug ip nat

Dynamic NAT

The following steps are necessary to configure Dynamic NAT on a Cisco router:

1. Use the ip nat inside command to configure the router's internal interface.

2. Use the ip nat outside command to configure the router's external interface.
3. Specify the range of public IP addresses that will be dynamically accessed by computers on the private network using the appropriate netmask.
4. Use an access control list to define a group of Private IP addresses for address translation
5. Map the access control list with the range of public IP addresses to be accessed dynamically.

Description	Command
Define the Router's internal interface	Router(config)#interface g0/0
Configure NAT inside a command to the router's internal interface	Router(config-if)#ip nat INSIDE
Define the Router's external interface	Router(config-if)#interface se0/3/0
Configure NAT outside command to the router's interface	Router(config-if)#ip nat OUTSIDE
Configure a pool to specify the range of Public IP addresses to be accessed dynamically {In this illustration we shall give a	Router(config)#ip nat pool TESTING 197.0.116.6 197.0.116.10 netmask 255.255.255.0

114

range of 5 addresses} with appropriate subnet mask/netmask.	
Configure a standard access control list (ACL)and specify the private network meant to access the public address. {In this illustration the address on the private network is 10.0.0.0/24}	Router(config)#access-list 6 permit 10.0.0.0 0.0.0.255
Allow the access list permissions to the range of Public IP addresses meant to be accessed via the internet.	Router(config)ip nat inside source list 6 pool TESTING

After configuring static NAT, you must be able to validate the setup.

We can use the following commands to validate the NAT translations:

Description	Command
To view basic IP address translation information	Router#show ip nat translation
To clear dynamic translation	Router# clear ip nat translation *

To view information about the total number of active translations	Router#show ip nat statistics
To clear statistics from any past translations	Router#clear ip nat statistics
To view NAT operation and display information about each packet the router translates	Router#debug ip nat
To view NAT events on specific IP addresses permitted by access-list	Router#debug ip nat 6

Port Address Translation (PAT)

The following steps are necessary to configure Dynamic NAT on a Cisco router:

1. Use the ip nat inside command to configure the router's internal interface.
2. Use the ip nat outside command to configure the router's external interface.
3. Specify the range of public IP addresses that will be dynamically accessed by computers on the private network using the appropriate netmask.
4. Use an access control list to define a group of Private IP addresses for address translation

5. Map the access control list with the range of public IP addresses to be accessed dynamically with NAT overload

Description	Command
Define the Router's internal interface	Router(config)#interface g0/0
Configure NAT inside a command to the router's internal interface	Router(config-if)#ip nat INSIDE
Define the Router's external interface	Router(config-if)#interface se0/3/0
Configure NAT outside command to the router's interface	Router(config-if)#ip nat OUTSIDE
Configure a pool to specify the range of Public IP addresses to be accessed dynamically {In this illustration we shall use one public IP address as the range} with appropriate subnet mask/netmask.	Router(config)#ip nat pool TESTING 197.0.116.6 197.0.116.6 netmask 255.255.255.0
Configure a standard access control list (ACL)and specify the private network meant to access the public address. {In	Router(config)#access-list 6 permit 10.0.0.0 0.0.0.255

this illustration the address on the private network is 10.0.0.0/24}	
Allow the access list permissions to the range of Public IP addresses meant to be accessed via the internet using the **overload** keyword	Router(config)ip nat inside source list 6 pool TESTING overload

After configuring static NAT, you must be able to validate the setup. We can use the following commands to validate the NAT translations:

Description	Command
To view basic IP address translation information	Router#show ip nat translation
To clear dynamic translation	Router# clear ip nat translation *
To view information about the total number of active translations	Router#show ip nat statistics
To clear statistics from any past translations	Router#clear ip nat statistics
To view NAT operation and display information about each packet the router translates	Router#debug ip nat

To view NAT events on specific IP addresses permitted by access-list	Router#debug ip nat 6

Comparison between Static NAT and Port Address Translation

Understanding the distinctions and benefits of these two strategies (Static NAT and Port Address Translation) becomes critical as organizations attempt to find the optimal balance between network security, resource management, and seamless connection.

Let's look at the distinctive features of Static NAT and PAT.

Static NAT	Port Address Translation (NAT Overload)
Inside Local and Inside Global, addresses are mapped one-to-one.	Many Inside Local addresses can be linked to a single Inside Global address.
In the translation procedure, only IPv4 addresses are used.	In the translation procedure, IPv4 addresses and TCP or UDP source port numbers are used.
Each inside host that connects to the outside network must have a unique Inside Global address.	Many inside hosts accessing the outside network can share a single unique Inside Global address

Advantages of Network address translation

Network Address Translation (NAT) offers various benefits that help modern networks run more efficiently and securely.

Here are some of the main benefits of using network address translation:

1. NAT allows numerous devices on a private network to share a single public IP address. This contributes to the conservation of the restricted pool of public IP addresses, which is especially important given the depletion of IPv4 numbers.

2. Security and privacy: NAT functions as a firewall by concealing devices' internal IP addresses from the public internet. External entities can only see the NAT router's public IP address, which adds a layer of protection and secrecy to the internal network.

3. Simplified Network Design: NAT makes it easier to manage internal IP address assignments. Private IP addresses can be used on internal networks without requiring coordination with the worldwide Internet Assigned Numbers Authority (IANA).

4. Address Space Segmentation: NAT allows an organization's network to employ private IP address ranges (such as those described in RFC 1918). This address space separation aids in the separation of internal resources and network segments from the public internet.

5. Protocol Compatibility: NAT supports a variety of network protocols, including TCP, UDP, and ICMP. Because of this compatibility, most apps and services can operate normally even while traveling over NAT.

6. Load Balancing: Load balancing is supported by some advanced NAT implementations by spreading incoming traffic among numerous internal servers. This can help to improve the performance and availability of internal network-hosted services.

7. Cost-effective: NAT avoids the requirement for a company to purchase a large number of public IP addresses for internal devices. This cost-cutting benefit is especially relevant for organizations and institutions with a large number of devices but limited IP address allocations.

8. Mobility Support: When devices with private IP addresses travel across networks, NAT allows them to connect to the internet by using the gateway/router's public IP address, providing continuous connectivity.

Disadvantages of Network address translation

While Network Address Translation (NAT) has many advantages, it also has significant drawbacks and restrictions.

The following are the major disadvantages of employing NAT:

1. Peer-to-Peer Communication Issues: Because NAT affects the IP addresses and port numbers in packet headers, it might cause problems with certain peer-to-peer applications and services. As a result, it becomes difficult to create direct connections between devices on various private networks, hurting applications such as online gaming, video conferencing, and file sharing.

2. Complex Configuration: Configuring NAT can be difficult, especially in big and intricate network configurations. Organizations may face challenges such as port forwarding, static NAT mappings, and managing multiple NAT devices, which can be difficult to handle successfully.

3. NAT introduces additional processing costs, resulting in increased network latency. Real-time applications that are sensitive to delays, such as VoIP (Voice over Internet Protocol) calls and online gaming, may be impacted.

4. Limited Scalability: In networks with a high number of devices, NAT might become a bottleneck. The NAT device may struggle to handle the volume of translations required as the number of connected devices increases, thus compromising network performance.

5. Dependence on Public IP Addresses: Some apps or services may require public IP addresses to function properly, hence bypassing the NAT. In such instances, businesses may be required to assign public IP addresses to specific devices, which reduces the benefits of IP address conservation provided by NAT.

6. Complex Troubleshooting: When problems emerge in a network using NAT, troubleshooting can become more difficult due to IP address and port number translation. It may be difficult to pinpoint the source of connectivity issues, resulting in lengthier resolution times.

7. Lack of End-to-End Connectivity: NAT violates the internet's end-to-end concept, which encourages direct connection between hosts without the need for intermediaries. Some forms of direct communication between hosts on separate networks become impossible with NAT in place.

8. IPv6 Transition Difficulties: As the globe transitions to IPv6 due to the expiration of IPv4 addresses, switching from NAT to IPv6 may necessitate greater labor and expenditure.

Review Exercise

1. The network topology below shows computers on the internal network of 192.168.10.0/24 and the public address as 215.145.200.0/29. R1 is meant to perform network address translation and simulate the public network.

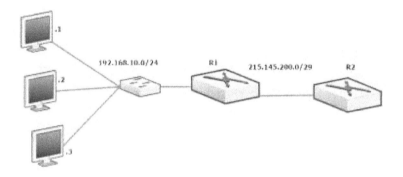

For this illustration, we shall use Packet tracer as a simulation software: The configuration R1 network address translation is as follows:

Before preceding with NAT configuration ensure you have configured IP addresses as follows based on the packet tracer topology:

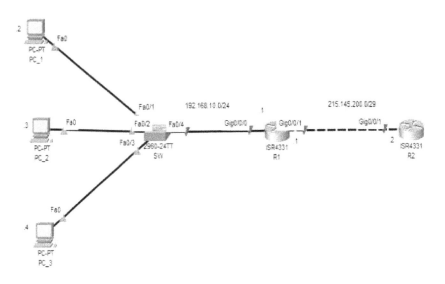

R1(config)#int g0/0/0
R1(config-if)#ip address 192.168.10.1 255.255.255.0
R1(config-if)#no shutdown
R1(config-if)#int g0/0/1
R1(config-if)#ip address 215.145.200.1 255.255.255.248
R1(config-if)#no shutdown

R1(config-if)#ip dhcp excluded-address 192.168.10.1
R1(config)#ip dhcp pool NETWORK_A
R1(dhcp-config)#network 192.168.10.0 255.255.255.0
R1(dhcp-config)#default-router 192.168.10.1
R1(dhcp-config)#end
R1#write
Building configuration...
[OK]

R2(config)#int g0/0/1
R2(config-if)#ip address 215.145.200.2 255.255.255.248
R2(config-if)#no shutdown

CONFIGURATIONS

```
R1(config)#int g0/0/0
R1(config-if)#ip nat INSIDE
R1(config-if)#int g0/0/1
R1(config-if)#ip nat OUTSIDE
R1(config-if)#ip nat inside source static 192.168.10.2 215.145.200.1
R1(config)#ip nat inside source static 192.168.10.3 215.145.200.1
R1(config)#ip nat inside source static 192.168.10.4 215.145.200.1
R1(config)#end
R1#write
Building configuration...
[OK]
```

Required:

a) Configure and verify Static NAT for IPv4 taking note of the three End devices.

Command Interpretations

int g0/0/0:

This command enters the configuration mode for the GigabitEthernet0/0/0 interface.

ip nat INSIDE:

This command designates the GigabitEthernet0/0/0 interface as an inside NAT interface. Inside interfaces are typically connected to the internal/private network.

int g0/0/1:

This command enters the configuration mode for the GigabitEthernet0/0/1 interface.

ip nat OUTSIDE:

This command designates the GigabitEthernet0/0/1 interface as an outside NAT interface. Outside interfaces are typically connected to the external/public network.

ip nat inside source static 192.168.10.2 215.145.200.1:

This command statically maps the private IP address 192.168.10.2 to the public IP address 215.145.200.1. This means that traffic coming from 192.168.10.2 will always be translated to 215.145.200.1 when leaving the network.

Testing whether the PCs can Access R2~From PC-2

```
Command Prompt

Cisco Packet Tracer PC Command Line 1.0
C:\>ping 215.145.200.2

Pinging 215.145.200.2 with 32 bytes of data:

Reply from 215.145.200.2: bytes=32 time<1ms TTL=254
Reply from 215.145.200.2: bytes=32 time<1ms TTL=254
Reply from 215.145.200.2: bytes=32 time<1ms TTL=254
Reply from 215.145.200.2: bytes=32 time<1ms TTL=254

Ping statistics for 215.145.200.2:
    Packets: Sent = 4, Received = 4, Lost = 0 (0% loss),
Approximate round trip times in milli-seconds:
    Minimum = 0ms, Maximum = 0ms, Average = 0ms

C:\>|
```

NAT Translation Verification Commands

R1#show ip nat translations

Pro	Inside global	Inside local	Outside local	Outside global
icmp	215.145.200.1:10	192.168.10.2:10	215.145.200.2:10	215.145.200.2:10
icmp	215.145.200.1:11	192.168.10.2:11	215.145.200.2:11	215.145.200.2:11
icmp	215.145.200.1:12	192.168.10.2:12	215.145.200.2:12	215.145.200.2:12
icmp	215.145.200.1:5	192.168.10.4:5	215.145.200.2:5	215.145.200.2:5
icmp	215.145.200.1:6	192.168.10.4:6	215.145.200.2:6	215.145.200.2:6
icmp	215.145.200.1:7	192.168.10.4:7	215.145.200.2:7	215.145.200.2:7
icmp	215.145.200.1:8	192.168.10.4:8	215.145.200.2:8	215.145.200.2:8
icmp	215.145.200.1:9	192.168.10.2:9	215.145.200.2:9	215.145.200.2:9
---	215.145.200.1	192.168.10.4	---	---

R1#show ip nat statistics

Total translations: 1 (3 static, 4294967294 dynamic, 0 extended)

Outside Interfaces: GigabitEthernet0/0/1

Inside Interfaces: GigabitEthernet0/0/0

Hits: 24 Misses: 28

Expired translations: 28

b) Configure and verify Dynamic NAT for IPv4 using a pool of three public addresses.

CONFIGURATIONS
R1(config)#ip nat pool ICT 215.145.200.1 215.145.200.3 netmask 255.255.255.248
R1(config)#access-list 10 permit 192.168.10.0 0.0.0.255
R1(config)#ip nat inside source list 10 pool ICT
R1(config)#end
R1#write
Building configuration...
[OK]

Command Interpretations

CONFIGURATIONS
R1(config)#ip nat pool ICT 215.145.200.1 215.145.200.3 netmask 255.255.255.248
R1(config)#access-list 10 permit 192.168.10.0 0.0.0.255
R1(config)#ip nat inside source list 10 pool ICT
R1(config)#end
R1#write
Building configuration...
[OK]

ip nat pool ICT 215.145.200.1 215.145.200.3 netmask 255.255.255.248:

This command defines a NAT pool named "ICT" with a range of IP addresses from 215.145.200.1 to 215.145.200.3, with a subnet mask of 255.255.255.248. This pool will be used to translate internal private IP addresses to public IP addresses.

access-list 10 permit 192.168.10.0 0.0.0.255:

This command creates an access control list (ACL) numbered 10, permitting traffic from the internal network with the subnet 192.168.10.0/24. This ACL will be used to identify which traffic should be subjected to NAT.

ip nat inside source list 10 pool ICT:

This command associates the previously created ACL (number 10) with the NAT pool "ICT". It instructs the router to perform NAT translation on traffic matching the criteria specified in ACL 10 using the IP addresses defined in the NAT pool "ICT

NAT Translation Verification Commands

```
R1#show ip nat translation
Pro Inside global    Inside local    Outside local    Outside global
icmp 215.145.200.1:1  192.168.10.3:1  215.145.200.2:1  215.145.200.2:1
icmp 215.145.200.1:2  192.168.10.3:2  215.145.200.2:2  215.145.200.2:2
icmp 215.145.200.1:3  192.168.10.3:3  215.145.200.2:3  215.145.200.2:3
icmp 215.145.200.1:4  192.168.10.3:4  215.145.200.2:4  215.145.200.2:4
icmp 215.145.200.2:1  192.168.10.2:1  215.145.200.2:1  215.145.200.2:1
icmp 215.145.200.2:2  192.168.10.2:2  215.145.200.2:2  215.145.200.2:2
icmp 215.145.200.2:3  192.168.10.2:3  215.145.200.2:3  215.145.200.2:3
icmp 215.145.200.2:4  192.168.10.2:4  215.145.200.2:4  215.145.200.2:4
icmp 215.145.200.3:1  192.168.10.4:1  215.145.200.2:1  215.145.200.2:1
icmp 215.145.200.3:2  192.168.10.4:2  215.145.200.2:2  215.145.200.2:2
icmp 215.145.200.3:3  192.168.10.4:3  215.145.200.2:3  215.145.200.2:3
icmp 215.145.200.3:4  192.168.10.4:4  215.145.200.2:4  215.145.200.2:4
```

R1#show ip nat statistics
Total translations: 8 (0 static, 8 dynamic, 8 extended)
Outside Interfaces: GigabitEthernet0/0/1
Inside Interfaces: GigabitEthernet0/0/0
Hits: 6 Misses: 12
Expired translations: 4
Dynamic mappings:
-- Inside Source
access-list 10 pool ICT refCount 8
 pool ICT: netmask 255.255.255.248
     start 215.145.200.1 end 215.145.200.3
     type generic, total addresses 3 , allocated 2 (66%), misses 0

c) Configure and verify Port Address Translation (NAT Overload).

CONFIGURATIONS

R1(config-if)#ip nat pool ICT 215.145.200.1 215.145.200.3 netmask 255.255.255.248

R1(config)#access-list 10 permit 192.168.10.0 0.0.0.255

R1(config)#ip nat inside source list 10 pool ICT overload

R1(config)#end

R1#write

Building configuration...

[OK]

Command Interpretations

ip nat pool ICT 215.145.200.1 215.145.200.3 netmask 255.255.255.248:

This command defines a NAT pool named "ICT" with a range of IP addresses from 215.145.200.1 to 215.145.200.3, with a subnet mask of 255.255.255.248. This pool will be used to translate internal private IP addresses to public IP addresses.

access-list 10 permit 192.168.10.0 0.0.0.255:

This command creates an access control list (ACL) numbered 10, permitting traffic from the internal network with the subnet 192.168.10.0/24. This ACL will be used to identify which traffic should be subjected to NAT.

ip nat inside source list 10 pool ICT overload:

This command configures NAT overload. It associates the previously created ACL (number 10) with the NAT pool "ICT". The keyword "overload" indicates that multiple private IP addresses will be translated to a single public IP address (PAT). This allows multiple devices with private IP addresses to share a single public IP address for outbound traffic.

NAT Translation Verification Commands

```
R1#show ip nat translation
Pro  Inside global      Inside local      Outside local      Outside global
icmp 215.145.200.1:1024192.168.10.2:5     215.145.200.2:5    215.145.200.2:1024
icmp 215.145.200.1:1025192.168.10.2:6     215.145.200.2:6    215.145.200.2:1025
icmp 215.145.200.1:1026192.168.10.2:7     215.145.200.2:7    215.145.200.2:1026
icmp 215.145.200.1:1027192.168.10.2:8     215.145.200.2:8    215.145.200.2:1027
icmp 215.145.200.1:1028192.168.10.4:5     215.145.200.2:5    215.145.200.2:1028
icmp 215.145.200.1:1029192.168.10.4:6     215.145.200.2:6    215.145.200.2:1029
icmp 215.145.200.1:1030192.168.10.4:7     215.145.200.2:7    215.145.200.2:1030
icmp 215.145.200.1:1031192.168.10.4:8     215.145.200.2:8    215.145.200.2:1031
icmp 215.145.200.1:5  192.168.10.3:5      215.145.200.2:5    215.145.200.2:5
icmp 215.145.200.1:6  192.168.10.3:6      215.145.200.2:6    215.145.200.2:6
icmp 215.145.200.1:7  192.168.10.3:7      215.145.200.2:7    215.145.200.2:7
icmp 215.145.200.1:8  192.168.10.3:8      215.145.200.2:8    215.145.200.2:8


R1#show ip nat statistics
Total translations: 12 (0 static, 12 dynamic, 12 extended)
Outside Interfaces: GigabitEthernet0/0/1
Inside Interfaces: GigabitEthernet0/0/0
Hits: 18  Misses: 24
Expired translations: 12
Dynamic mappings:
-- Inside Source
access-list 10 pool ICT refCount 12
 pool ICT: netmask 255.255.255.248
     start 215.145.200.1 end 215.145.200.3
     type generic, total addresses 3 , allocated 1 (33%), misses 0
```

2. A border router's active NAT translations need to be examined by Mr. Timudu the network administrator. Which of the following commands will do the task?

A. Router#Show ip nat statistics

B. Router#Show ip nat translations

C. Router#Clear ip nat translations

D. Router#debug ip nat translations

Explanation

A. Router#Show ip nat statistics: This command provides statistics about NAT translations, such as how many packets have been translated, but it does not display the active translations themselves.

B. Router#Show ip nat translations: This command is used to display the active NAT translations on the router. It will show you the mappings between internal private IP addresses and external public IP addresses.

C. Router#Clear ip nat translations: This command is used to clear the NAT translation table, removing all existing translations. It does not display the active translations.

D. Router#debug ip nat translations: This command enables debugging for NAT translations, which means it will show real-time information about NAT translations as they occur, but it doesn't provide a static display of existing translations like option B does.

Therefore, the correct command for examining active NAT translations is option B: Router#Show ip nat translations.

3. A corporation builds its network so that packets going to the Internet are translated through a NAT-capable router, while PCs on the internal network are given IP addresses by DHCP servers. What type of NAT allows the router, when the PCs send packets through the router to the Internet, to populate the translation table from a pool of unique public addresses?

A. Dynamic NAT

B. Address Resolution Protocol (ARP)

C. Port Address Translation (PAT)

D. Static NAT

Explanation

PAT, also known as NAT overload, maps multiple private IP addresses to a single public IP address by using different source port numbers. This allows multiple devices with private IP addresses to share a single public IP address when accessing resources on the Internet

NOTE:

When configuring Dynamic NAT and NAT overload ensure you have designated appropriate interfaces as INSIDE and OUTSIDE using the following commands:

ip nat INSIDE:

This command designates the GigabitEthernet0/0/0 interface as an inside NAT interface. Inside interfaces are typically connected to the internal/private network.

ip nat OUTSIDE:

This command designates the GigabitEthernet0/0/1 interface as an outside NAT interface. Outside interfaces are typically connected to the external/public network.

Chapter 7: IPv4 Routing Protocols

IPv4 Routing is an important component of internetwork communication that is in charge of directing data packets to their destinations using IP addresses. Each network-connected device is assigned a unique IP address, which serves as its virtual identity tag. Routing protocols come into play when data is transferred from one device to another, determining the most effective path for the information to take through the network. These protocols ensure that data packets take the shortest, quickest, or most reliable path feasible, increasing information flow throughout the vast network of interconnected devices. IPv4 Routing ensures that our digital world remains linked and accessible by facilitating the seamless exchange of information that has become an essential part of our daily lives.

The following is a summary of the fundamental concepts of IPv4 routing protocols.

Routing and Routers

Routing is the process of moving data packets from a source network to a destination network. Data packets are routed by routers, and network devices, based on the IP addresses of their final destinations. Routers examine the routing table to determine the best packet-forwarding route.

Routing Tables

Routing tables are essential router components that store information about network destinations and the next-hop routers. During the packet forwarding process, the routing table is queried to find the proper outgoing interface and next-hop router for each packet.

Routing Protocols

Routing protocols are collections of rules and methods used by routers to exchange routing information and construct routing tables. They enable routers to automatically share network topology information, allowing them to make educated routing decisions. Static Routing, Routing Information Protocol (RIP), Open Shortest Path First (OSPF), and Enhanced Interior Gateway Routing Protocol (EIGRP) are examples of common routing protocols.

Routing Metrics

Routing protocols use metrics to find the optimum path for packet forwarding. Metrics describe the cost, dependability, or performance of a certain route. Common measurements include hop count, bandwidth, latency, and load. The routing protocol analyses these metrics to determine the best path for packet transmission.

Static versus Dynamic Routing

Routing can be achieved through static or dynamic routing. Static routing involves manually configuring the routing table on each router, specifying the next-hop router for each network destination. Dynamic routing, on the other hand, utilizes routing protocols to automate the exchange of routing information and dynamically update the routing tables based on network changes.

It's important to note that routing protocols allow routers to communicate routing information and construct routing tables, enabling efficient and reliable packet transfer. Understanding routing protocols is essential for network administrators and engineers since it allows efficient network design, optimization, and troubleshooting.

Configuration and maintenance of routing tables are critical responsibilities in network management to ensure efficient and correct routing. Routing table configuration and maintenance are critical for optimal network performance. Let's look at routing table configuration and maintenance in depth using the notable routing protocols.

7.1 Static Routing

Static routing is a mechanism for manually configuring the paths that data packets take from one network device to another. It allows network administrators to manually configure a fixed route (or path) for data to travel, which remains intact unless the administrator changes it.

Consider it similar to putting up road signs or directions for a certain destination. Instead of the network devices determining the best way dynamically, static routing predetermines the path and does not change unless someone makes a conscious adjustment to the routing parameters. It is crucial to remember that static routing is best suited for smaller, simpler networks with predictable traffic patterns and few network components. Dynamic routing protocols, which allow network devices to communicate with each other to identify the optimum paths automatically, are commonly employed in larger and more complicated networks.

Types Static Routing

The following are the types of static routes.

1. **Standard static route**

   A standard static route is a form of static routing configuration that is commonly used in computer networks. It entails setting a single static route for all traffic destined for a certain network or server manually.

   The network administrator defines the following parameters in a standard static route:

   a) **Host or Destination Network**: This is the network address or IP address of the destination host to which data packets should be delivered.

   b) **Next-Hop Address**: The IP address of the next device (router) on the way to the destination is the next-hop address. It acts as the gateway through which data packets should be sent to their destination.

   c) **Outgoing Interface**: Some setups allow you to provide the outgoing interface directly instead of the next-hop IP address. The router will utilize its routing table to choose the appropriate next hop in this case.

   d) When a data packet arrives at a router, it compares the destination IP address to the static routes that have been established. If the destination IP address matches any of the static routes, the router forwards the packet using the information in the static route configuration.

If no match is found in the static routes, the router will attempt to find a route using alternative methods, such as dynamic routing protocols or a default route.

2. Default static route

A "default route" is a special setting in the network configuration of a router that determines the path to take when no specified route is available for a certain destination IP address. It acts as a default gateway, allowing data to be sent to other networks or the internet when the device lacks a more specified route to a specific destination. It essentially functions as a "catch-all" route, guaranteeing that data can be transferred even when the destination is not expressly known to the device.

Sure, let's take an example to clarify the concept of a default route: Assume you are a delivery driver for a corporation that delivers packages to various residences in a town. You have a list of precise addresses (routes) to which you must deliver packages. You organize your itinerary accordingly, visiting each address depending on the information you have.

However, one day your employer sends you a package bearing an address you've never seen before and that isn't on your list. You have no idea where to distribute it because you have no explicit instructions for that place.

In this case:

The routing table of a network device, such as a router or a computer, is represented by the delivery list with specific addresses.

The known addresses on the list are specific routes in the routing table that tell the device where to forward data to specified destinations.

The package with the strange address contains inbound data that the gadget must send to a place it has never encountered before.

The **"default route"** now comes into play:

Your supervisor provides you with the following default instruction: "If you don't know where to deliver a package, just drop it off at the main post office."

The main post office operates as the "default gateway" for your delivery in this scenario. If you can't find the address on your list (special route), you always have the option of taking the item to the main post office (default route) for additional handling and delivery.

The default route serves as a safety net, ensuring that data can still be delivered even if the destination is unknown or not defined in the routing table.

3. Floating static route

A "floating static route" is a routing arrangement in which a static route is assigned a greater administrative distance or metric than another route. This technique is widely used to construct a backup route that becomes active only when the primary route fails.

Routing tables are used by routers to determine the best path for data packets to take to their destinations. A static route is a routing table item that has been manually set to specify the path to a single target network. However, in some cases, having a backup route that takes effect when the primary route fails may be useful.

That's where the concept of a floating static route comes in:
Assume you own a small firm with two internet service providers (ISPs) providing internet access to your location. You want to make sure that your network stays connected to the internet even if one of the ISPs goes down. You decide to create a floating static route to do this.

In this scenario:
Principal Route (Higher Priority): ISP A is your principal internet provider, and its connection is quicker and more dependable. In your router, you set up a static route that directs all outgoing internet traffic to ISP A's gateway.

Backup Route (Lower Priority): ISP B is your secondary internet provider, and it acts as a backup if ISP A fails. You install another static route in your router that directs all outgoing internet traffic to ISP B's gateway, but this route has a greater administrative distance or metric. The higher the administrative distance, the less desirable it is for it to be the preferred route.

Let's take a look at how the floating static route works:

Normally, your router will use the primary route with ISP A (the one with the shortest administrative distance) to forward all data packets to the internet. This path is recommended since it has a higher metric, resulting in faster and more efficient data transmission.

However, if ISP A goes down or becomes unreachable, your router will notice the problem. Because the primary route is no longer available, the router will switch to the backup route with ISP B (higher administrative distance). This floating static route becomes active, allowing your workplace network to maintain internet connectivity through the backup ISP.

Network managers can improve network resiliency and redundancy by installing floating static routes, guaranteeing that data can still be sent to its destination even if the primary route fails. This strategy improves network resilience and reduces downtime, which is critical for businesses that rely significantly on internet connection for day-to-day operations.

Next-Hop Option Concept

The next hop in a static route can be indicated by an IP address, an exit interface, or both.

The way the destination is supplied results in one of three types of static routes:

1. **Next-hop path**- Only the IP address of the following hop is supplied.

2. **The static route that is directly connected to** the router exit interface is the only one listed.

3. **Completely stated static route**- The IP address of the next hop and the exit interface are supplied.

Standard Static Route Configuration using Next-hop-path option

Assumptions:

Router IP address: 172.16.0.1

Destination network: 192.168.10.0/24

Next-hop gateway: 172.16.0.2

Description	Command
Get into the router's global configuration mode	Router(config)#
Specify the IP route command followed by the destination network address and its subnet mask and finally the IP address of the neighbor router also known as the next hop	Router(config)#ip route 192.168.10.0 255.255.255.0 172.16.0.2
Return to Privileged Exec mode	Router(config)#end
Saves the configuration to the router's NVRAM, to ensure that	Router#copy running-config startup-config

the static route remains in place after a reboot.	

Default static Route Configuration

Assumptions:

Router IP address: 10.0.0.1

Default gateway (next-hop IP): 10.0.0.2

Description	Command
Get into the router's global configuration mode	Router(config)#
To match any network address, use the ip route command with the network address 0.0.0.0 and the subnet mask 0.0.0.0.	Router(config)#ip route 0.0.0.0 0.0.0.0 10.0.0.2
Return to Privileged Exec mode	Router(config)#end
Saves the configuration to the router's NVRAM, to ensure that the static route remains in place after a reboot.	Router#copy running-config startup-config

The command ip route 0.0.0.0 0.0.0.0 10.0.0.2 installs the default static route. It instructs the router to redirect all traffic with no defined destination (0.0.0.0/0) to the next-hop gateway at IP address 10.0.0.2.

Floating static Route Configuration

Assumptions:

Router IP address: 172.16.10.1

Primary next-hop gateway: 172.16.11.2

Backup next-hop gateway: 172.16.12.3

Administrative distance for the backup route: 50

Description	Command
Get into the router's global configuration mode	Router(config)#
Add a major static route by instructing the router to forward all traffic with a destination not specific (0.0.0.0/0) to the main next-hop gateway at the address 172.16.11.2.	Router(config)# ip route 0.0.0.0 0.0.0.0 172.16.11.2
Add a floating static route (backup route) by instructing the router to send all incoming traffic with no specified destination (0.0.0.0/0) to the backup next-hop gateway at IP address 172.16.12.3 but with a greater administrative distance of 50.	Router(config)# ip route 0.0.0.0 0.0.0.0 172.16.12.3 50
Return to Privileged Exec mode	Router(config)#end

Saves the configuration to the router's NVRAM, to ensure that the static route remains in place after a reboot.	Router#copy running-config startup-config

A floating static route indicates that the backup route will only be employed if the primary route fails or becomes inaccessible.

7.2 Routing Information Protocol (RIP)

RIP routing protocol is straightforward and distance-vector-based. The best route to a destination network is found by counting the number of hops (distance between routers). Every router exchanges routing tables with each of its neighbors, who then exchange them with each of theirs. RIP is appropriate for networks that are modest to medium in size. However, because of its delayed convergence and inability to effectively handle complicated topologies, it is constrained in bigger networks.

The use of RIP to determine the shortest path between two routers in a small office network with numerous interconnected routers is an illustration of how it works.

Concept of Administrative distance

The administrative distance (AD) is a measure of how reliable routing data that a router receives from a neighboring router is. An administrative distance is an integer between 0 and 255, where 255 indicates that no traffic will pass over the route and 0 is the most trusted.

The AD is the first item a router evaluates if it receives two updates with the same remote network listed in them. If one of the advertised routes has a lower AD than the other, the route with the lowest AD will be chosen and added to the routing table.

Route Source	Default Administrative Distance (AD)
Connected Interface	0
Static Route	1
RIP	120
EIGRP	90
External EIGRP	170
OSPF	110
Unknown	255 {This route will never be used}

RIP categories

RIP version 1 (RIPv1) and RIP version 2 (RIPv2) are the two versions of RIP that can be employed. Since RIP version 1 only employs classful routing, any device connected to the network must have the same subnet mask. This is because RIP version 1 does not transmit updates with subnet mask data attached. Prefix routing is a feature of RIP version 2 that communicates subnet mask data along with route updates. The term for this is classless routing.

RIP version 1	RIP version 2
It does not send subnet masks in routing updates because it is a classful protocol.	It sends subnet masks in routing updates since it's a classless protocol.
It communicates with neighbors through broadcast	It enables peer communication through multicast.
Does not support authentication	Supports authentication
Does not support Variable Length Subnet Mask (VLSM)	Supports Variable Length Subnet Mask (VLSM)

The following traits apply to RIP:

1. Every 30 seconds, the whole routing table is sent out.
2. It employs hop counts as a measurement and has a 15-hop count cap.
3. High convergence time is present.

Configuring RIP

When a router first powers on, it detects the linked networks and adds them as connected routes (indicated in the routing table by the letter C). The routing table will be broadcast via UDP port 520 when RIP is enabled. This broadcast update will be received by any nearby routers with RIP enabled, and they will all add the updated routes to their routing tables. These neighbors will each transmit their routing tables in turn. The routing tables throughout the network will converge as a result.

Let's set up RIP on two Cisco routers as a basic demonstration. We'll make an assumption to have Router X and Router Y, which are directly connected through their Fast Ethernet interfaces and have the following IP addresses:

Router X

FastEthernet0/0: 192.168.10.1/24

Router Y

FastEthernet0/0: 192.168.10.2/24

Description	Command
On RX configure router rip global configuration command to enable RIP globally.	RX(config)#router rip
Change the router's version to [version 2].	RX(config-router)#version 2
Configure a directly connected network on RX where IP Address 192.168.10.1 belongs and any other network(s) visible in the routing table.	RX(config-router)#network 192.168.10.0
Prevent Automatic summarization to disable sending a subnet mask of the classful	RX(config-router)#no auto-summary

boundary instead of an actual subnet mask.	
On RY configure router rip global configuration command to enable RIP globally.	RY(config)#router rip
Change the router's version to [version 2]	RY(config-router)#version 2
Configure a directly connected network on RY where IP Address 192.168.10.2 belongs and any other network(s) visible in the routing table.	RY(config-router)#network 192.168.10.0
Prevent Automatic summarization to disable sending a subnet mask of the classful boundary instead of an actual subnet mask.	RY(config-router)#no auto-summary
To view networks remotely learned.	RY#show ip route
To view the settings a specific protocol uses to send and receive updates, the metrics it employs, and the networks it promotes.	RY#show ip protocol

In a network with this configuration, routers will communicate over the network to share RIP updates. Based on the number of hops, RIP will choose the best route to various networks. In contrast to more recent routing protocols like OSPF or EIGRP, RIP has limitations in terms of scalability and convergence speed. As a result, RIP is no longer frequently utilized in sophisticated or sizable networks.

7.3 Enhanced Interior Gateway Routing Protocol (EIGRP)

EIGRP is a hybrid routing protocol that combines aspects of both link-state and distance-vector protocols. The best route to a location is chosen using a metric based on bandwidth, delay, reliability, and load. Despite being a Cisco proprietary protocol, EIGRP is frequently utilized in Cisco-based networks. It delivers quick convergence and effective utilization of network resources. An example of EIGRP would be a network that mostly employs Cisco hardware, where EIGRP is used to optimize routing decisions and improve network performance.

EIGRP Features

The following characteristics of a distance vector protocol are inherited by EIGRP:

1. Its default maximum hop count is 100, however, it can be raised to 255.

2. It makes use of a rumor-routing technique

3. It uses loop-avoiding strategies like split horizon.

It inherits the following features of a link-state protocol:

1. It finds nearby neighbors and periodically checks about them(status).

2. It sends information when a change happens rather than regularly.

The Diffusing Update Algorithm (DUAL) is used by EIGRP to determine the best route to remote networks.

The key characteristics of DUAL are:

1. Support of VLSMs

2. Dynamically recovers missing routes.

3. Finding the backup route and using it if the primary route is lost.

4. It finds alternatives if a route is lost and no backup route is found.

5. Uses various metrics to determine the best routes.

The quick EIGRP convergence time is a result of DUAL. EIGRP's convergence time may be the quickest of all the routing protocols. All EIGRP routers keep a copy of the network topology, which gives room for fast convergence.

A router will simply search the topology table for a backup route if the best route goes down.

In a scenario where a backup route is not found in the topology table, the neighbor routers will be consulted by a given router to find an alternate path.

The following metrics are used by EIGRP to calculate the best path:

1. Bandwidth (also called path bandwidth value)

2. Delay (also called cumulative line delay)

3. Load

4. Reliability

The two metrics that are utilized to determine the best path are bandwidth and delay, but it is possible to modify them to also take into account the other two metrics. Keep in mind that two routers configured to use different metrics will not form an adjacency.

Summary of an EIGRP Communication packet

1. **Hello:** Used to identify neighbors. Used to locate neighbors. Periodic multicasts are sent out.

2. **Update:** Primarily used to advertise routes and only transmitted as multicasts when something has changed.

3. **Ack:** Used to confirm receipt of a new update. Ack is an empty Hello packet. It uses UDP and is always unicast.

4. **Query:** After all routes to a target have failed, to locate alternate routes

5. **Reply:** It is transmitted in response to inquiry packets to tell the originator not to recompute the route because there are feasible successors. Response packets are always sent in a single direction to the query's creator.

EIGRP prefers gathering and keeping as much data about the network as possible. A router saves information about each neighbor in a table known as the Neighborship or Neighbor table as it acquires knowledge about neighbors and establishes an adjacency.

After adjacencies are developed, neighbors exchange routing tables. These tables provide details about remote networks and their connections to them. The Topology table is the place where information is kept.

Information received from the neighbor entails the following:

1. Remote network's address
2. The remote network's subnet mask
3. Next hop to the remote network
4. Cost to the remote network

Configuring EIGRP

Enabling EIGRP on routers, identifying the participating interfaces, and fine-tuning various parameters to regulate the protocol's behavior are all necessary steps in configuring it. EIGRP also offers load balancing, authentication, and route summarization, giving network managers the tools, they need to create robust, high-performance networks. This introduction examines the fundamental components of the EIGRP setup, which forms the basis of resilient and adaptable routing infrastructures.

Let's set up EIGRP on two Cisco routers as a basic demonstration. We'll make an assumption to have Router X and Router Y, which are directly connected through their FastEthernet interfaces and have the following IP addresses:

Router X

FastEthernet0/0: 192.168.10.1/24

Router Y

FastEthernet0/0: 192.168.10.2/24

Description	Command
Access the global configuration mode of RX and Enable EIGRP	RX(config)#router eigrp 600

using an Autonomous System (AS)number between 1-65535.	
Configure a directly connected network on RX where IP Address 192.168.10.1 belongs to and any other network(s) visible in the routing table.	RX(config-router)#network 192.168.10.0
Prevent Automatic summarization to disable sending a subnet mask of the classful boundary instead of an actual subnet mask.	RX(config-router)#no auto-summary
Access the global configuration mode of RY with the same AS number as that of RX.	RY(config)#router eigrp 600
Configure a directly connected network on RX where IP Address 192.168.10.2 belongs and any other network(s) visible in the routing table.	RY(config-router)#network 192.168.10.0
Prevent Automatic summarization to disable sending a subnet mask of the classful	RY(config-router)#no auto-summary

boundary instead of an actual subnet mask.	
To view networks remotely learned.	RY#show ip route
To view the settings a specific protocol uses to send and receive updates, the metrics it employs, and the networks it promotes.	RY#show ip protocol

7.4 Open Shortest Path First (OSPF)

OSPF is a link-state protocol that communicates with nearby routers to exchange data on the status of the network link. Each router builds a full map of the network, enabling it to determine the shortest way to a destination using parameters like bandwidth and cost. For larger and more complicated networks, such as enterprise networks, OSPF is a good fit because of its great scalability and speedy convergence. For instance, OSPF allows routers to efficiently interact and identify the best paths for data transfer in a big business network with numerous routers and switches.

It uses the concept of areas. To better manage routing update traffic, a network administrator might divide the routing domain into distinct areas. A link state is data that describes the state of a link. The cost, prefix length, and network prefix are all included in the link-state data.

OSPF Components

The components of all routing protocols are similar. To share route information, they are all using routing protocol messages. The messages contribute to the development of data structures, which are then handled by a routing algorithm.

To keep accurate information about the network, these packets are used to find nearby routers and to share routing data.

Five different types of packets are used by routers running OSPF to exchange messages and transmit routing information:

Five different types of packets are used by routers running OSPF to exchange messages and transmit routing information:

1. Hello packet: Finds neighbors and creates connections between them
2. Database description packet: Checks to see if routers have their databases synchronized.
3. Link-state request packet-Particular link-state records from router to router are requested
4. Link-state update packet-Sends link-state records upon specific request
5. Link-state acknowledgment packet-Recognizes other packet types

Link-State Operation

OSPF routers reach a state of convergence by completing a general link-state routing process to maintain routing information. The steps of link-state routing that a router completes are as follows:

1. Establish Neighbor Adjacencies
2. Exchange Link-State Advertisements

3. Build the Link State Database

4. Execute the SPF Algorithm

5. Choose the Best Route

Concept of Multi-Area

An OSPF area is a collection of routers that share the same link-state information in their LSDBs. OSPF can be implemented in one of two ways, as follows: Single-Area OSPF - All routers are in one area; best practice is to use area 0. Multiarea OSPF - OSPF is implemented using multiple areas, hierarchically; all areas must connect to the backbone area (area 0).

With multiarea OSPF, the hierarchical-topology design provides the following benefits:

1. Smaller routing tables - Because there are fewer entries in the routing table, tables are smaller. This is because network addresses can be compiled across regions. Route summarization is not by default turned on.

2. Reduced link-state update overhead - Processing and memory needs are reduced when multiarea OSPF is designed with fewer, smaller areas.

3. Reduced frequency of SPF calculations -The effects of a topology change are localized within an area by multiarea OSPF. Since LSA flooding ends at the area boundary, the impact of routing updates is minimized.

Categories of Multi-Area Components

Upon occurrence of database synchronization, two routers are regarded as being adjacent. It's crucial to keep in mind that if the following criteria are not met, neighbors will not establish an adjacency:

1. Area ID
2. Subnet
3. Hello and dead timers
4. Authentication (if configured)

Configuring OSPF

When configuring OSPF, the steps entail creating OSPF areas, assigning networks to specific areas, and adjusting OSPF parameters to meet the needs of the network.

Let's set up OSPF on two Cisco routers as a basic demonstration. We'll assume to have Router X and Router Y, on the backbone area directly connected through Fast Ethernet interfaces with the following IP addresses:

Router X

FastEthernet0/0: 192.168.10.1/24

Router Y

FastEthernet0/0: 192.168.10.2/24

Description	Command
Access global configuration mode of RX and Enable OSPF	RX(config)#router ospf 600

using Autonomous System (AS)number between 1-65535.	
Configure a directly connected network on RX where IP Address 192.168.10.1 belongs and any other network(s) visible in the routing table to the backbone Area. The wildcard mask usage disables sending a subnet mask of the classful boundary instead of an actual subnet mask.	RX(config-router)#network 192.168.10.0 0.0.0.255 area 0
Access global configuration mode of RX and Enable OSPF using Autonomous System (AS)number between 1-65535. {It's not a must to use the same AS number as with the case with EIGRP}	RY (config)#router ospf 1200
Configure a directly connected network on RX where IP Address 192.168.10.1 belongs and any other network(s) visible in the routing table to the	RY(config-router)#network 192.168.10.0 0.0.0.255 area 0

backbone Area. The wildcard mask usage disables sending a subnet mask of the classful boundary instead of an actual subnet mask.	
To view networks remotely learned.	RY#show ip route
To view the settings a specific protocol uses to send and receive updates, the metrics it employs, and the networks it promotes.	RY#show ip protocol

In summary, routing protocols are essential because they govern how routers communicate and decide what information to forward. Small networks can benefit from the distance-vector protocol RIP (Routing Information Protocol). Due to its sluggish convergence, it employs hop count as its metric and has a constrained ability to scale.

Large enterprise networks frequently employ the link-state protocol OSPF (Open Shortest Path First). It uses a link-state database to determine the shortest path, allowing for quick convergence and effective routing. Scalability is provided via OSPF's hierarchical design with areas, which also lessens the impact of topology changes.

EIGRP (Enhanced Interior Gateway Routing Protocol) combines link-state and distance-vector features. It supports VLSM (Variable Length Subnet Masking), provides quick convergence, and makes efficient use of the available resources. Especially in Cisco systems, EIGRP is well suited for medium to large-scale networks. Administrators must take into account factors such as network size, complexity, convergence time, and vendor compatibility when selecting a routing protocol to guarantee the best performance and dependability of their network infrastructure.

Review Exercise

1. The network topology below shows two computers connected on two different networks (192.168.10.0/30 and 192.168.10.8/30) shared by a common network between the two routers (192.168.10.4/30).

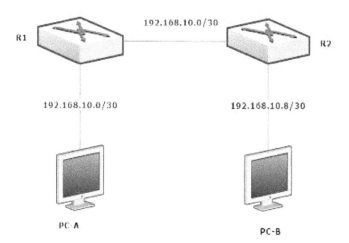

Required:

Configure a standard static route to enable PC-A to communicate with PC-B.

For this illustration, we shall use Packet tracer as a simulation software: The configuration R1, R2, PC-A, and PC-B is as follows: Before preceding with Static Route configuration ensure you have configured IP addresses as follows based on the packet tracer topology:

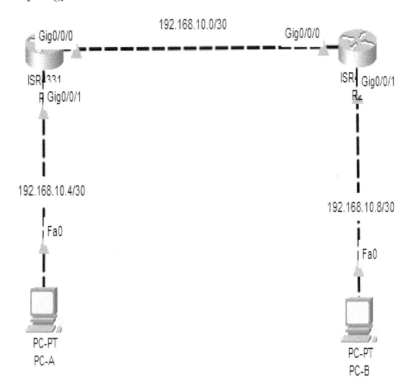

```
Router(config)#hostname R1
R1(config)#
R1(config)#int g0/0/0
R1(config-if)#ip address 192.168.10.1 255.255.255.252
R1(config-if)#no shutdown

R1(config-if)#int g0/0/1
R1(config-if)#ip address 192.168.10.5 255.255.255.252
R1(config-if)#no shutdown
R1(config-if)#end
R1#write
Building configuration...
[OK]

Router(config)#hostname R2
R2(config)#
R2(config)#int g0/0/0
R2(config-if)#ip address 192.168.10.2 255.255.255.252
R2(config-if)#no shutdown

R2(config-if)#int g0/0/1
R2(config-if)#ip address 192.168.10.9 255.255.255.252
R2(config-if)#no shutdown
R2(config-if)#end
R2#write
Building configuration...
[OK]
```

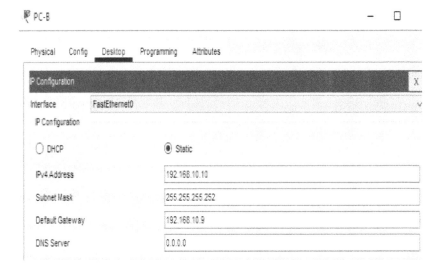

Standard Static Route From R1

R1(config)#ip route 192.168.10.8 255.255.255.252 192.168.10.2
R1(config)#do write
Building configuration...
[OK]

Interpretations

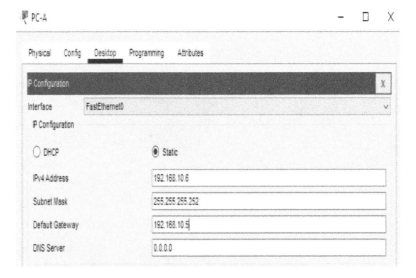

ip route: This indicates that the command is related to IP routing.**192.168.10.8:** This is the destination network or host IP address. **255.255.255.252:** This is the subnet mask for the destination network.

192.168.10.2: This is the next-hop IP address, indicating where packets should be forwarded to reach the destination network.

In summary, this command instructs the device to send any traffic destined for the network or host with the IP address range 192.168.10.8/30 (which includes IP addresses from 192.168.10.8 to 192.168.10.11) to the next-hop IP address 192.168.10.2 for further routing.

Standard Static Route From R2

```
R2(config)#ip route 192.168.10.4 255.255.255.252 192.168.10.1
R2(config)#do write
Building configuration...
[OK]
```

Interpretations

ip route: This specifies that an IP route configuration is set to.192.168.10.4: This is the destination network or host IP address.255.255.255.252: This is the subnet mask for the destination network.192.168.10.1: This is the next-hop IP address, indicating where packets should be forwarded to reach the destination network.

In essence, this command instructs the device to route any traffic destined for the network or host with the IP address range 192.168.10.4/30 (which includes IP addresses from 192.168.10.4 to 192.168.10.7) to the next-hop IP address 192.168.10.1 for further routing.

Connectivity Between PC-A &PC-B

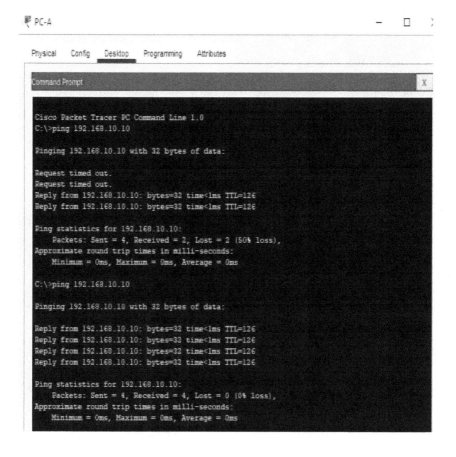

2. The command ip route 0.0.0.0 0.0.0.0 196.61.20.26 is used by a network administrator to configure a router. Which of these statements BEST describes the purpose of the command?

A. To send every packet to the computer with the IP address 196.61.20.26.

B. To deliver data packets intended for the network to the computer with the IP address 196.61.20.26 0.0.0.0

C. To offer a route to forward packets when the routing table is missing a route

D. To include a dynamic route in the routing table for the destination network 0.0.0.0.

Explanation

This command, ip route 0.0.0.0 0.0.0.0 196.61.20.26, is commonly used to configure a default route on a router. A default route is used when the router doesn't have a specific route in its routing table for a particular destination. Instead, it forwards packets to the specified next-hop IP address (in this case, 196.61.20.26) for further routing.

So, option C best describes the purpose of this command: "To offer a route to forward packets when the routing table is missing a route."

3. A default route is characterized by which of the following statements?

A. **It indicates the gateway IP address that the router uses to route any packets in which a static route is not specified.**

B. Compared to the original dynamic routing system, it has a greater administrative distance configured.

C. It sends several static routes to a single destination address using a single network address.

D. It supports a route found by the dynamic routing protocol

Explanation

A default route, often denoted as 0.0.0.0/0, specifies the gateway IP address that a router uses to route packets when it doesn't have a specific route in its routing table for the destination network of the packet. This is essentially a catch-all route that handles any packets for which a more specific route is not defined.

Chapter 8: IPv4 Security

To protect data and network integrity, IPv4 brings specific problems and vulnerabilities that must be fixed. A comprehensive strategy is required to secure IPv4-based networks due to the rising number of internet-connected devices and the ongoing evolution of cyber threats. To reduce threats like unauthorized access, data interception, and denial-of-service attacks, IPv4 security includes several techniques, such as authentication, encryption, access controls, and intrusion detection. Understanding and putting into practice strong security measures are crucial to fostering a safe and secure digital environment for individuals, companies, and societies at large given the extensive reliance on IPv4 for communication and data transfer.

8.1 IPv4 addressing vulnerabilities

Networks are susceptible to several security concerns and threats due to IPv4 addressing issues. For security measures to be put in place, it is essential to comprehend these vulnerabilities.

The following are examples of IPv4 addressing flaws:

1. **IP Spoofing**: IP spoofing includes changing a packet's originating IP address to make it appear as though it came from a reliable source.

   Attacks such as denial-of-service (DoS), man-in-the-middle attacks, and bypass of access controls can all be launched using this method. Network devices can be duped by forged IP addresses, compromising data integrity and confidentiality.

2. **IP Address Scanning**: It is a technique used by attackers to find active hosts in a network. They learn more about prospective targets for further exploitation by searching for open ports and services. Attackers can use it to learn more about network devices, find security holes, and launch attacks.

3. **IP Address Exhaustion**: The exhaustion of IPv4 addresses is a serious issue because there aren't many IPv4 addresses left. Organizations may use ineffective workarounds like network address translation (NAT) to share a finite number of public IP addresses as a result of exhaustion, which can cause address shortages. This may affect network scalability, obstruct effective communication, and make IP address administration more challenging.

4. **IP Address Misconfiguration**: Internal network resources may unintentionally be exposed to external attackers due to incorrectly configured IP addresses. For instance, open ports or improperly set firewall rules may permit unauthorized access to sensitive systems. To reduce these risks, it is essential to install access controls, configure IP addresses correctly, and review and update configurations frequently.

5. **IP Address Hijacking**: When an attacker unlawfully seizes control of a genuine IP address range, it is known as IP address hijacking. This may occur through some techniques, including DNS hijacking or the exploitation of shoddy network protocols. Attackers can intercept network communication once it has been

taken over, carry out assaults, or pose as legitimate network entities.

6. **IP Address Blacklisting**: IP addresses may occasionally be blacklisted as a result of questionable or malicious behavior. When an IP address is connected to spamming, virus distribution, or other harmful activities, blacklisting may take place. This may result in the filtering or blocking of valid traffic, which would disrupt operations and harm the reputation of the network.

7. **IP Address Disclosure:** Some factors, such as incorrectly set up web servers, unprotected APIs, or the transmission of network traffic, might result in the accidental disclosure of IP addresses. This data can be used by attackers to locate possible targets, conduct reconnaissance, or execute targeted attacks against particular IP addresses or network ranges.

Organizations and network administrators can find potentially weak spots and implement the necessary security measures by having a solid grasp of common IPv4 addressing issues. To reduce these vulnerabilities and safeguard networks from potential threats, it is advised to install strong network security controls, regular system updates and patches, network traffic monitoring, and access controls.

Network security methods

To safeguard against potential attacks and guarantee the integrity of network communication, IPv4 addresses and networks must be secured. The following techniques can be used to enhance IPv4 address safety in a network setup

a) Network Segmentation: By dividing the network into smaller, isolated portions, network segmentation helps to reduce the possible attack surface. To isolate their network traffic and prevent illegal access, corporations can, for instance, build distinct VLANs (Virtual Local Area Networks) for various departments, such as finance, human resources, and operation

b) Access Control Lists (ACLs): Network traffic is filtered using ACLs according to predefined criteria. Administrators can manage which IP addresses or ranges are permitted or refused access to particular network resources by configuring ACLs on routers or firewalls. For instance, a company might configure ACLs to restrict access to sensitive information or essential systems to a small number of trusted IP addresses.

c) Network Address Translation (NAT): With the use of NAT, numerous devices can share a small pool of public IP addresses by converting private IP addresses to public IP addresses. To make it harder for attackers to target particular devices, this approach conceals internal IP addresses from external networks, adding an extra layer of security.

d) DHCP Snooping: A security measure known as DHCP snooping stops unauthorized DHCP servers from distributing IP addresses over the network. Network devices can examine DHCP traffic and confirm the reliability of DHCP servers thanks to this. For instance, Cisco switches allow DHCP snooping, which guards against potential threats like IP address spoofing and assists in preventing rogue DHCP servers from giving IP addresses.

e) Intrusion Detection and Prevention Systems (IDS/IPS): IDS/IPS systems can identify and stop a variety of attacks, including those that target IP addresses, by monitoring network traffic for suspicious behavior. These systems can be set up to notify administrators or launch automatic responses when suspicious or malicious traffic is found. One open-source IDS/IPS system that can be used to defend networks from attacks on IPv4 addresses is Snort.

Organizations can significantly improve the security of their IPv4 addresses and networks in general by putting these strategies into practice and combining them with other security measures like robust authentication systems, encryption, and ongoing monitoring. It's crucial to customize these strategies under particular network requirements, industry best practices, and the changing threat landscape.

8.2 Access Control List (ACL) and Firewall Rules

Assume you have multiple rooms and would wish to manage who can enter each room and what they can do. You want to safeguard your valuables by preventing illegal access. In the context of data communication, all these can be achieved through Access Control Lists (ACLs) and Firewall rules.

Access Control Lists (ACLs)

Access Control Lists (ACLs) are sets of rules that specify what network traffic can enter or exit a particular network device, such as a switch or router. ACLs can be compared to a nightclub bouncer who verifies everyone's identification before allowing them entry.

ACLs operate by looking at network-transmitted data packets. The source and destination of each packet are disclosed in the information contained within. Based on a predetermined set of rules, ACLs use these details to determine whether to allow or refuse the packet.

You may, for example, construct an ACL rule that only accepts incoming traffic from a set of IP addresses or completely prohibits a set of network traffic categories. ACLs can also be used to manage network outbound traffic. ACLs essentially function as a filter that allows some packets to flow while denying others.

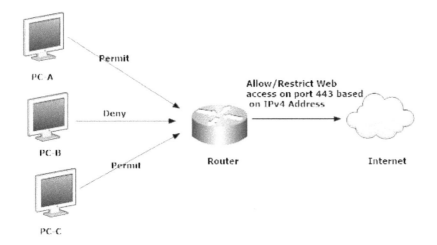

ACLs are needed by routers to identify traffic for the following tasks:

1. To improve network performance, reduce network traffic
2. Controlling the flow of traffic
3. Provide network access with a minimal level of security
4. Sort traffic according to its type
5. To allow or prohibit access to network services, screen hosts
6. Give particular types of network traffic priority

Firewall Rules

A firewall is a network security device that acts as a barrier between your network and the outside world, much like the walls of your house protect you from the outside elements. Firewall rules are the instructions you give to the firewall to determine what network traffic is allowed or blocked.

Firewalls operate by inspecting network traffic and applying rules to determine if a packet should be allowed or blocked. These rules can be based on various factors such as the source and destination IP addresses, port numbers, protocol types, and more. You could, for instance, set up a firewall rule that only enable incoming web traffic on port 80 (the default HTTP port) to get to your web server. All other incoming traffic would be blocked. Simila to the restriction of incoming connections, rules can be set up to prevent access to particular websites or services.

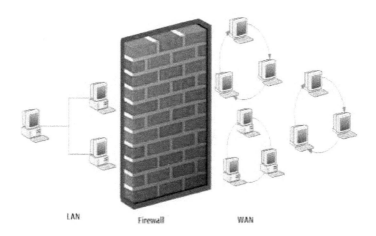

LAN   Firewall   WAN

For network security, firewall rules are crucial because they assist in preventing malware from spreading, hostile assaults, and unauthorized access.

Types of IPv4 ACLs

There are two types of IPv4 ACLs

1. Standard ACLs - The only criteria used to allow or prohibit packets using standard ACLs is the source IPv4 address.

2. Extended ACLs - The source and destination IPv4 addresses, the protocol type, the source and destination TCP or UDP ports, and other factors are taken into account by extended ACLs when deciding whether to allow or reject packets.

Numbered and Named ACLs

Numbered ACLs

Standard ACLs have a number between 1 and 99, or 1300 to 1999, while extended ACLs have a number between 100 and 199, or 2000 to 2699.

R1(config)# access-list ?

<1-99> IP standard access list

<100-199> IP extended access list

<1100-1199> Extended 48-bit MAC address access list

<1300-1999> IP standard access list (expanded range)

<200-299> Protocol type-code access list

<2000-2699> IP extended access list (expanded range)

Router(config)# access-list

Named ACLs

The best way to configure ACLs is with named ACLs. In particular, standard and extended ACLs can be named to convey information about the ACL's function. For instance, designating an extended ACL FTP-FILTER is much better than having an ACL with a value like 100.

As demonstrated in the following example, a named ACL is created using the IP access-list global configuration command.

R1(config)# ip access-list extended XYZ

R1(config-ext-nacl)# permit tcp 192.168.11.0 0.0.0.255 any eq telnet

R1(config-ext-nacl)# permit tcp 192.168.11.0 0.0.0.255 any eq ftp

R1(config-ext-nacl)#

ACL Operation

ACLs specify the set of rules that provide additional control for packets entering inbound interfaces, relaying across the router, and leaving outbound interfaces. ACLs can be set up to apply to both incoming and outgoing traffic. Note that packets coming from the router itself are unaffected by ACLs.

Before a packet is forwarded to an outgoing interface, an incoming ACL filters it. Because it avoids the cost of routing lookups if the packet is dropped, an incoming ACL is effective.

Regardless of the inbound interface, an outgoing ACL filters packets after they have been routed.

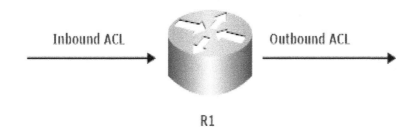

Inbound ACL   Outbound ACL

R1

Standard Access List Configuration

Scenario:

Let's assume for this example that you have a modest network with a router and three devices linked to it. To allow communication from one

IP address and block traffic from another, you need to set up a standard access list on the router.

Device X: 192.168.0.10

Device Y: 192.168.0.20

Device Z: 192.168.0.30

Router interface connected to Device X: GigabitEthernet0/1

Router interface connected to Device Y: GigabitEthernet0/2

Router interface connected to Device Z: GigabitEthernet0/3

Objective: Permit traffic from Device X (192.168.0.10) and prevent traffic from Device Y (192.168.0.20) using the standard access list on the router's interface connected to Device Z(GigabitEthernet0/3).

Description	Command
Get into the global configuration mode of the router	RZ(config)#
Allow traffic from Device X and block traffic from Device Y, using a standard access list.	RZ(config)# access-list 6 permit 192.168.0.10 RZ(config)# access-list 6 deny 192.168.0.20
Apply the access list to the router's Device Z interface.	RZ(config)# interface GigabitEthernet0/3 RZ(config-if)# ip access-group 6 in
Check/Verify the access list configuration.	RZ(config-if)# exit RZ(config)# exit RZ# show access-lists

Please be aware that this is only a basic example to show how to set up a typical access list. You might need to build extensive security measures with the help of various access lists and more complicated requirements in real-world circumstances. Before implementing the setup in a production environment, make sure you fully test the configuration and comprehend the impact of access list rules on your network traffic.

Extended Access List Configuration

Scenario:

Let's use a small network corporation as an example. The business has a router that connects to the internet and internal devices. The business wishes to set up an extended access list on the router to permit particular inbound internet traffic and restrict access to particular internal services.

WAN interface of the Router connected to the internet: FastEthernet0/0 (Public IP: x.x.x.x)

LAN interface of the router linked to the internal network: FastEthernet0/1 (IP: 192.168.10.1)

Objective: Set up the router's extended access list to only allow HTTP and HTTPS traffic from the Internet to a specific internal web server (192.168.10.50) and block all other incoming Internet traffic to the internal network.

Description	Command
Get into the global configuration mode of the router	Router(config)#
Create an extended access list to allow HTTP and HTTPS communication to the internal web server (192.168.10.50) and to block all other incoming traffic from the Internet.	Router(config)# access-list 120 permit tcp any host 192.168.10.50 eq 80 Router(config)# access-list 120 permit tcp any host 192.168.10.50 eq 443 Router(config)# access-list 120 deny ip any any
Apply the access list to the FastEthernet0/0 WAN interface of the router.	Router(config)# interface FastEthernet0/0 Router(config-if)# ip access-group 120 in
Check/Verify the access list configuration.	Router (config-if)# exit Router (config)# exit Router # show access-lists

This illustration uses access list number 120. The first two lines allow incoming TCP traffic on ports 80 (HTTP) and 443 (HTTPS) from any source IP address to the internal web server (192.168.10.50). The final line blocks any additional IP traffic, regardless of source or destination.

Please be aware that this is a simple illustration example. In real-world settings, you might need to design extensive security policies with more complicated requirements and various access lists. Always extensively test the configuration to make sure it satisfies your security requirements without interfering with genuine traffic before implementing it in a production environment.

8.3 Port Security

When we talk about port security, we're talking about a collection

of settings and options intended to increase safety and manage access to certain switch ports. A local area network (LAN) is made up of several connected devices, and network switches are the means through which data can be transferred between them.

A network switch's port security primarily aims to safeguard against potential security threats and assaults and to stop unauthorized devices from connecting to the network.

A network switch's port security typically includes the elements and characteristics listed below:

1. **MAC Address Filtering**: Each device plugged into a switch port has a Media Access Control (MAC) address that is noted. Network administrators can decide which MAC addresses are granted or refused access to particular switch ports by using MAC address filtering. Any device trying to connect to a secured port with an unauthorized MAC address may be prevented.

2. **Port Lockdown**: A switch port is permanently associated with a particular MAC address through port lockdown. By doing this, even if the original device is disconnected, no other device can

connect to that port. It adds another level of protection from illegal access.

3. **DHCP Snooping**: Snooping on the Dynamic Host Configuration Protocol (DHCP) helps stop malicious DHCP servers from giving networked devices IP addresses. It makes sure that only approved DHCP servers can give devices IP addresses.

4. **VLAN Membership**: The network can be logically divided with the help of virtual LANs (VLANs). Specific switch ports can have their VLAN membership restricted by port security, limiting the VLANs that their linked devices can access.

5. **Storm Control**: Storm control stops broadcast, multicast, or unidentified unicast storms that might interfere with networks or be exploited maliciously. To prevent the network from becoming overloaded, it restricts the rate at which such traffic is forwarded.

6. **Port Security Violation Actions**: Administrators can set the switch to perform specified tasks when a port security violation occurs, such as closing the port, alerting the user, or reporting the incident.

Scenario: Securing a Network Switch Port Using Port Security

Assume you are a network administrator tasked with setting port security on a network switch to bar illegal devices from connecting to the network. Your network switch connects to a crucial server through a single port (Port 1) on the switch. This port should only be accessible to particular devices with known MAC addresses.

Description	Command
Get into the global configuration mode of Switch X and Switch Y	Switch(config)#
On the switch, enable port security on port 1	Switch(config)# interface port FastEthernet0/1 Switch(config-if)#switchport mode access Switch(config-if)#switchport port-security
On Port 1, set the Maximum Allowed MAC Addresses to 1 since only 1 device is authorized to access.	Switch(config)# interface port FastEthernet0/1 Switch(config-if)#switchport port-security maximum 1
Configure MAC addresses on port 1 to be dynamically learned through Sticky	Switch(config)# interface port FastEthernet0/1 Switch(config-if)#switchport port-security mac-address sticky
Define the action that the switch should take in case of unauthorized access.	Switch(config)# interface port FastEthernet0/1 Switch(config-if)#switchport port-security violation shutdown
To Display details for the FastEthernet0/1 interface	Switch # Show port-security interface FastEthernet0/1

Network managers can improve access control, lower the possibility of malicious activity or unauthorized access, and preserve the overall security and integrity of the network infrastructure by implementing these port security measures.

8.4 DHCP Attack

Using attack tools like Gobbler, a DHCP starvation attack seeks to deny service to clients connected to the network.

Port security can be used to effectively mitigate DHCP starvation attacks because Gobbler uses a unique source MAC address for each DHCP request sent.

Preventing DHCP spoofing attacks requires more protection. Gobbler can be set up to utilize the Ethernet address specified in the DHCP payload as the source ethernet address instead of the MAC address of the actual device. As a result, port security would be useless because the source MAC address would be trustworthy.

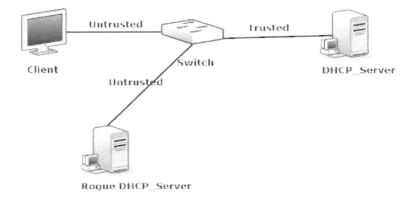

By utilizing DHCP snooping on trusted ports, DHCP spoofing attacks can be reduced.

Filtering and rate-limiting of DHCP traffic on untrusted ports are accomplished through DHCP snooping.

1. Trusted sources are devices under administrative control such as switches, routers, and servers

2. Trusted interfaces (e.g., trunk links, server ports) must be set to trusted explicitly.

3. Untrusted sources are devices outside the network and all configured access ports

DHCP Snooping Configuration

Scenario:

Assume for this example that you are a network administrator for a business that wants to protect its network from illegal DHCP servers and shield it from DHCP-related threats. To accomplish this, you choose to enable DHCP Snooping on your network switches.

Network Setup:

Switch X: Core switch with DHCP server connected to GigabitEthernet0/1

Switch Y: Access switch connected to Core Switch on GigabitEthernet0/2 with Client devices on Fast Ethernet 0/15-FastEthernet 0/20

Description	Command
Get into the global configuration mode of Switch X and Switch Y	SwitchX (config)# SwitchY (config)#
On both switches, turn on DHCP Snooping.	SwitchX (config)# ip dhcp snooping SwitchY (config)# ip dhcp snooping
Configure Gigabit Ethernet 0/1 connected on Switch X as trusted because DHCP server is connected to it.	SwitchX (config)#interface GigabitEthernet0/1 SwitchX (config-if)# ip dhcp snooping trust
Configure Gigabit Ethernet 0/1 connected on Switch Y as trusted because its connected to the Core Switch(X)	SwitchY (config)#interface GigabitEthernet0/1 SwitchY (config-if)# ip dhcp snooping trust
Configure ports {FastEthernet0/15-20} connected to client devices on both switch Y as untrusted.	SwitchY (config)#interface range FastEthernet0/15-20 SwitchY (config-if)#ip dhcp snooping limit rate 5
To verify configuration of the DHCP Snooping on each switch	SwitchY # show ip dhcp snooping

The IP dhcp snooping limit rate 5 command limits the number of DHCP messages that can be sent on untrusted ports to 5 per second. This aids in reducing the risk of DHCP-based attacks like DHCP flooding.

Review Exercise

1. A computer specialist made a variety of adjustments to fix the issue. A solution was eventually discovered after some unsuccessful attempts at solving the issue. What needs to be documented?

   A. Only the unsuccessful attempts, so that aspiring technicians can understand what to avoid trying.

   B. A breakdown of the issue and its resolution.

   C. Only the remedy since it addressed the issue.

   D. All that was done to fix the issue.

   ### Explanation

   Documenting both the issue and its resolution is essential for several reasons:

   ✓ It provides a comprehensive record for future reference, allowing technicians to understand the problem and its solution.

   ✓ It facilitates knowledge transfer within the team, ensuring that everyone is aware of the issue and how it was resolved.

   ✓ It helps in troubleshooting similar issues in the future by providing insights into what worked and what didn't.

   ✓ It serves as a historical record for tracking trends or recurring problems, which can inform preventive measures.

While documenting unsuccessful attempts can be valuable for learning purposes, it's equally important to document the final resolution to provide a complete picture of the issue and its ultimate solution.

2. A network technician is troubleshooting an email connection problem. Which of the following end-user questions will provide clear information to better define the problem?

   A. What sort of technology do you employ to deliver emails?

   B. When did you discover your email issue?

   C. What is the Size of the emails you attempted to send?

   D. Is your email operational right now?

   Explanation

   "When did you discover your email issue?" This question will help the technician understand the timeline of when the problem began, potentially identifying any recent changes or events that could be related to the email connection problem.

3. A networked PC can print to a nearby printer and ping other nearby computers, but it has problems connecting to the Internet. There are no problems with other PCs connected to the same network. What is the problem?

   A. The connection between the switch to which the PC is connected and the default gateway route is broken.

   B. The switchport's specified IPv4 address is wrong.

   C. There is no default route for the default gateway router.

D. The computer's default gateway is either missing or incorrect.

Explanation

The computer's default gateway is either missing or incorrect. This scenario indicates that the PC can communicate within the local network (printing to a nearby printer and pinging other nearby computers) but cannot access the internet, suggesting an issue with its gateway configuration

Chapter 9: IPv4 Troubleshooting

The backbone of the majority of networks is Internet Protocol version 4 (IPv4) which serves as the foundation for data flow across devices in the internetwork. Nevertheless, issues are bound to develop in even the most carefully planned networks: IP addresses collide, packets veer off, and services fail to connect. This chapter sets you in a good position to understand IPv4 troubleshooting, arming you with the information and methods to recognize, isolate, and remove these barriers successfully. We conduct a thorough investigation of typical problems and their fixes, giving you the knowledge and confidence to successfully negotiate the complexities of network troubleshooting

IPv4 Troubleshooting gives IT specialists the ability to keep safe and reliable network connections, which ultimately improves user experiences, operational effectiveness, and the overall success of businesses and individuals in the digital age.

The following are key reasons as to why mastering IPv4 troubleshooting is crucial:

1. **Sustaining Network Connectivity**: Network outages can cause an interruption in company operations, communication, and even interpersonal interactions in today's linked society. IPv4 troubleshooting ensures that devices can connect without interruption, reducing downtime and increasing productivity.

2. **Enhancing User Experience**: Online resources must be accessed quickly and consistently by users. By investigating IPv4-

related issues, network managers can find and fix issues that might worsen user experience, like sluggish website load times or dropped connections.

3. **Minimizing Business Impact**: Network outages or performance problems can cost businesses money and harm their reputations. Rapid and efficient IPv4 troubleshooting reduces the effects of such problems and aids organizations in maintaining operational continuity.

4. **Security and Data Protection**: Network abnormalities or weaknesses sometimes precede security breaches. IT experts can find and fix potential points of entry for cyberattacks by troubleshooting IPv4 network security issues and protecting critical data and systems.

5. **Optimizing Resource Utilization**: There are a limited number of network resources, such as IP addresses and bandwidth. By ensuring effective resource allocation and usage, avoiding waste, and improving overall network performance, IPv4 troubleshooting can help.

6. **Learning Network Dynamics**: One can gain a deeper understanding of how networks work by investigating IPv4 problems. The ability to understand the root causes of issues and execute workable remedies makes this knowledge useful for IT workers.

7. **Skill Development**: Critical abilities like problem-solving, analytical thinking, and attention to detail are honed by IPv4

troubleshooting. These abilities support professional development and apply to many IT professions.

8. **Supporting Remote Workforce**: Employees increasingly use network connectivity to access corporate resources as remote work becomes more common. Remote IPv4 troubleshooting enables IT professionals to deliver prompt help and preserve a fluid remote working environment.

9. **Network Evolution**: New services and technologies are integrated as networks develop. IT specialists who have experience troubleshooting IPv4 issues are better able to react to these changes and make sure there are no interruptions.

10. **Bolstering IT Reputation**: Faster problem resolution is a result of competent IPv4 troubleshooting, which shows the professionalism and knowledge of IT staff. As a result, confidence and trust are increased both within businesses and with clients.

Troubleshooting Process

Procedures for General Troubleshooting

Because networks, problems, and troubleshooting experience vary, troubleshooting can take a lot of time. Administrators with experience, however, are aware that employing an organized troubleshooting approach will reduce the total troubleshooting time.

As a result, systematic procedures should be used to direct the troubleshooting process. To reduce time lost due to inconsistent hit-and-miss troubleshooting, this calls for clearly defined and documented troubleshooting methods. These methods are not static, though. The methods used to troubleshoot a problem are not always the same or carried out in the same sequence.

To fix a problem, some troubleshooting techniques can be applied. The simplified three-stage logic flowchart for troubleshooting is shown below. To solve a network issue, though, a more thorough procedure might be more beneficial.

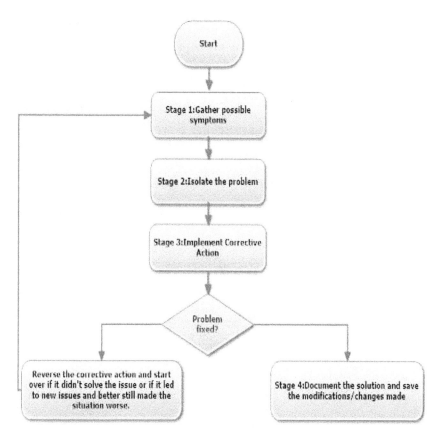

Seven-Step Troubleshooting Process

You can use the following streamlined seven-step troubleshooting procedure to address IPv4 network issues:

1. **Identify the Problem**

   This stage's objectives are to confirm the existence of an issue and then precisely identify it. Symptoms, such as a slow or unresponsive network, are frequently used to pinpoint problems. Network symptoms can manifest in a variety of ways, such as alarms from the network management system, console messages, and user complaints.

   To narrow the problem's potential causes to a more manageable number, it is crucial to research the situation while collecting symptoms. For instance, is the issue isolated to a single device, a collection of devices, or the entire network or subnet of devices? In an organization, issues are often documented as trouble tickets and given to network personnel. These tickets are made utilizing difficulty ticketing software, which keeps track of each ticket's development. Additional features of trouble ticketing software may include a self-service user portal for ticket submission, a searchable knowledge base for trouble tickets, remote control abilities for resolving end-user difficulties, and more.

2. **Gather Information**

   This process entails identifying the targets (i.e., hosts or devices) to be probed, gaining access to the targets, and gathering data.

Depending on the traits that are discovered, the technician may collect and record further symptoms at this stage.

Before collecting more network symptoms, get in touch with an administrator for the external system if the issue is beyond the organization's scope of control (for example, lost internet connectivity outside of the autonomous system).

3. **Analyze information**

   The root of the problem must be determined. The acquired data is processed and examined utilizing network baselines, network documentation, internet searches, organizational knowledge bases, and conversations with other technicians.

4. **Eliminate Possible Causes**

   If more than one cause is found, the list must be whittled down by eliminating some causes one at a time until the most likely cause is found. Experience with troubleshooting can help you swiftly rule out potential causes and pinpoint the most likely one.

5. **Develop Hypotheses**

   Based on the information acquired, come up with potential reasons for the problem.

   Take into account elements like incorrect settings, hardware malfunctions, or communication issues. When putting forth a plan at this point, troubleshooting experience is quite helpful.

6. **Test Hypotheses**

   It's critical to evaluate the problem's importance and impact before putting the solution to the test. Could the solution, for instance, negatively impact other processes or systems? The impact of the solution should be compared to how serious the issue is. For instance, it could be wiser to postpone implementing the update until the end of the workday if a crucial server or router needs to be taken offline for a sizable time. In some cases, a solution can be developed until the real issue is fixed.

Make a rollback strategy detailing how to swiftly undo a change. If the solution doesn't work, it might be essential to do this.

After putting the solution into practice, be sure the issue has been resolved. Sometimes a remedy causes an unanticipated issue. As a result, it's crucial to fully validate a solution before moving on to the next stage.

If the solution doesn't work, the failed solution is recorded, and the modifications are undone. The technician must now return to the information-gathering phase and identify the problem.

7. **Solve the problem**

Once the issue has been fixed, let the users and everyone else involved in the troubleshooting process know. The answer needs to be shared with the rest of the IT staff. The proper documentation of the root cause and solution will help future support professionals avoid and resolve issues of a similar nature.

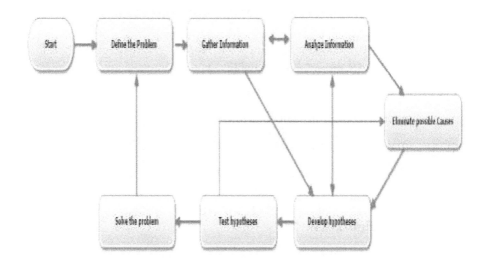

9.1: IP Addressing and Subnetting Issues

Solving IP addressing and subnetting problems is similar to putting together a jigsaw puzzle with some pieces that don't quite fit. It would be anarchy to attempt to deliver mail without house numbers or street names. These issues frequently appear when subnetworks collide like rush-hour traffic or when devices cannot locate one another owing to mismatched addresses. To resolve these problems, it is necessary to clear up address discrepancies and traffic congestion and make sure that each device is aware of its digital home and the lanes it should use.

9.1.1 Incorrect IP address configuration.

The term "incorrect IP address configuration" describes how network addresses, especially Internet Protocol (IP) addresses, are set up improperly. IP addresses are necessary for devices to communicate with one another within a network or over the internet. This misconfiguration may cause some connectivity problems and obstruct networked device functionality.

Scenario: Setup of a Home Network

Imagine you're building up a little home network with a few laptops, smartphones, and a printer. Instead of relying on your router's automatic assignment (DHCP), you choose to manually allocate IP addresses to each device.

Incorrect Configuration:

PC1:

IP Address: 172.16.1.10

Subnet Mask: 255.255.0.0

Default Gateway: 172.16.1.1

Smartphone:

IP Address: 192.168.0.100

Subnet Mask: 255.255.255.0

Default Gateway: 192.168.1.1 (Incorrect Gateway)

Printer:

IP Address: 192.168.100.30

Subnet Mask: 255.255.255.0

Default Gateway: 192.168.100.1

In this configuration, the default gateway of the smartphone is set to "192.168.1.1" rather than "192.168.0.1," which is the correct IP address of the network router.

Consequences:

1. Communication Issues: The smartphone won't be able to connect to the internet, communicate effectively with other networked devices, or submit print jobs to the printer.

2. Isolation: Due to the wrong gateway, there may be limited connectivity between the smartphone and other devices.

3. Network Resources: The smartphone won't be able to access network resources like shared files or streaming services run by other devices.

4. Printing Problems: Other devices can still print to the printer because its IP setup is correct, but the smartphone won't be able to connect to it.

5. Troubleshooting: Given that other devices are functioning properly, diagnosing the problem may be challenging.

Resolution

You would need to adjust the network settings on the smartphone to use the correct default gateway (192.168.0.1) to fix this. The smartphone should be able to communicate with other devices and use network resources without any problems when this adjustment is made.

You would need to adjust the network settings on the smartphone to use the correct default gateway (192.168.0.1) to fix this. The smartphone should be able to communicate with other devices and use network resources without any problems when this adjustment is made.

9.1.2 Subnet mask mismatches

Another common networking problem that can occur while configuring IP addresses within a network is subnet mask mismatches. For devices to determine whether other devices are on the same local network or require routing through a gateway to interact, subnet masks are essential in defining the boundaries of several subnets within a larger network.

Let's look at an illustration to comprehend subnet mask mismatches:

Scenario: Subnetting Small Office Home Office (SOHO) network

Put yourself in the position of an IT manager setting up a new office network. To efficiently manage network traffic, you choose to adopt subnetting. Sales and Marketing are your two departments. To improve organization and security, each department will be given its subnet.

Incorrect Configuration:

Marketing Subnet:

Subnet Address: 192.168.10.0

Subnet Mask: 255.255.255.192 (mistakenly set)

Sales Subnet:

Subnet Address: 192.168.10.32

Subnet Mask: 255.255.255.224

In this case, the Sales subnet's subnet address and mask are mistakenly set to "192.168.10.32" and "255.255.255.224" rather than the desired "192.168.10.64" and "255.255.255.192."

Consequences:

1. Incorrect Subnet Range: Devices in the Sales subnet will have IP addresses ranging from 192.168.10.33 to 192.168.10.62 as a result of the incorrect subnet mask, which overlaps with the IP range of the Marketing subnet.

2. Communication Issues: Sales subnet devices may have connectivity issues with those in the Marketing subnet as well as other parts of the network due to the overlapping IP address ranges.

3. Routing Confusion: The mismatched subnet mask may make it difficult for routers and switches to decide which paths should be used for data transmission.

4. Security Risk: The overlap in IP ranges may cause unwanted access to critical information and resources because devices that were supposed to be segregated from one another are now being reachable.

Resolution:

To establish a suitable separation between the two subnets, the network address of the sales subnet should be adjusted to "192.168.10.64" and the subnet mask to "255.255.255.192". Devices within each subnet will have unique IP ranges once the subnet mask has been fixed, and network communication will work as intended.

This example shows how a straightforward oversight in setting up subnet masks can result in challenging connectivity and security problems within a network. By logically segmenting devices into distinct subnets, proper subnetting ensures effective traffic management and improves network security.

9.1.3 Address conflicts (IP address duplication).

When two or more devices on a network are given the same IP address, IP address duplication takes place. Unique numerical identities known as IP (Internet Protocol) addresses are used to find and contact devices on a network. Multiple devices using the same IP address might cause network interruptions and communication issues.

To further understand this concept, let's look at a straightforward example:

Scenario: A small Network with IP Address Conflict

Consider a scenario in which your home network is connected to some devices, including a computer (Device A) and a printer (Device B).

When a device connects to the network, the network router serves as the DHCP (Dynamic Host Configuration Protocol) server and is in charge of allocating IP addresses to connected devices.

Initial Setup:

Device X (Computer): DHCP assigned IP address - 192.168.100.2

Device Y (Printer): DHCP assigned IP address - 192.168.100.3

IP Address Conflict:

Now suppose you manually set Device Y's IP address to correspond to Device X's address:

Printer device Y: IP address manually set: 192.168.100.2

Device X and Device Y currently share the same IP address (192.168.100.2). This kind of scenario leads to an IP address conflict.

Consequences:

1. Network Communication Issues: The router won't be able to distinguish between Device A and Device B when they try to communicate over the network because they both have the same IP address. This may lead to network instability, lost data, and broken connections.

2. Unpredictable Behavior: Some devices might occasionally have connectivity problems, and some network services might not work properly.

3. Unreliable Printing: Users may encounter difficulties printing consistently if Device Y is a printer or may encounter issues altogether.

Resolution:

You would need to modify one of the devices to use a separate, unique IP address to resolve the IP address conflict. By gaining access to the device's network settings and changing its IP setup, this can be accomplished. In this case, you could resolve the dispute by changing the printer's IP address back to its initial assignment (192.168.100.3).

IP address conflicts can happen for several reasons, including incorrect network device configuration, DHCP lease management problems, or human configuration errors. It's crucial to rely on DHCP for IP address assignment and to avoid manually configuring IP addresses unless essential to avoid these conflicts.

To prevent address conflicts that might disrupt communication and create problems while troubleshooting in larger networks, it is crucial to employ IP address management tools and to carefully organize the network.

9.2: Physical Layer Issues

Physical layer problems are like ghosts in the machinery; they cause havoc without leaving a trail. These problems relate to the physical part of technology, where frayed cables, incorrectly blinking lights, and loose connections resemble a mischievously assembled digital jigsaw. It's the time when your Ethernet wire plays hide-and-seek or your Wi-Fi signal disappears for a while. Getting your hands dirty with hardware, rolling up your sleeves, and ensuring sure the bits and bytes can move seamlessly from one device to another are all necessary for troubleshooting physical layer issues.

9.2.1 Cable connectivity problems

Cable connectivity problems are problems caused by flaws or interruptions in the actual cables that link devices together in a network. Data transmission and network dependability may be impacted by these issues, which may result in shaky or lost connections.

Let's examine this using an illustration:

Scenario: Connectivity issues with network cables

Imagine that you are in charge of IT for a tiny workplace that has a few computers and a server in the middle. Ethernet cables are used to connect each device to a network switch.

Initial Setup:

Computer X: Ethernet cable connected to the network switch.

Computer Y: Also, the Ethernet cable is connected to the network switch.

Server: Ethernet cable connected to the network switch.

Cable Disruption:

Users report having trouble accessing the server and having sporadic internet connectivity one morning. After doing some research, you discover that Computer X's Ethernet cable was accidentally kicked and only partially attached to the switch.

Consequences:

1. Computer X: It has trouble keeping a steady connection, which causes slow data transfer and sporadic disconnects.

2. Network Communication: As a result of Computer X's inability to communicate effectively, it is unable to contact the server, and other devices may be adversely affected by potential network congestion brought on by retransmitted data.

Troubleshooting and Resolution:

1. Physical Inspection: You locate the cable that was just partially detached and firmly reinstall it into the network switch port.

2. Testing: You check that Computer A can now communicate properly and access the server after you reconnect the wire.

3. Preventive Measures: You might think about employing cable management solutions to stop unintentional cable disconnections to prevent similar problems in the future.

Physical damage, subpar cable, slack connections, and improper cable usage are just a few of the causes of cable connectivity issues. IT specialists often visually analyze cables, test connections with various devices, and utilize cable testers to find defects to troubleshoot these issues. To enable smooth and dependable data transmission in bigger networks, adequate cable labeling, management, and routine maintenance become crucial.

In this case, resolving the cable connectivity issue needed a mix of rapid discovery, hands-on assistance, and proactive actions to maintain the network's stability.

9.2.2 Network interface card (NIC) failures.

Consider operating a small business with a network of computers that lets your staff members exchange files, work together on projects, and access the internet. A Network Interface Card (NIC) is a device that each computer has that connects it to the network. One day, you begin getting complaints from workers in a certain office space. The shared files are unavailable to them, and they occasionally have connectivity problems.

Your analysis reveals that the machines there are certainly experiencing network issues. The loading of files takes an eternity, and occasionally the connection is lost entirely. You isolate a specific machine and make an effort to troubleshoot. You make sure the Ethernet wire is properly inserted into the computer and the network outlet by checking it. To rule out any problems there, you even replace the cable. But the issue still exists.

After that, you choose to upgrade the NIC driver on the problematic computer since you suspect a software bug may be to blame for the problem. Sadly, the issue still exists even after updating the driver. You now believe the NIC itself may be experiencing a hardware issue.

You choose to replace the NIC from the problematic computer with a functional NIC from another computer in a different part of the office to confirm your suspicions. Once you've done this, you discover that the troublesome machine is now in perfect working order, and the problems are now with the computer where you installed the questionable NIC.

This test demonstrates that the NIC is indeed defective and is the root cause of the network outages. All network-related issues in that part of the workplace mysteriously disappear when you swap out the damaged NIC with a new one. Employees may easily access data, collaborate, and browse the internet without encountering any issues.

This example shows how NIC failure can affect a particular area of a network, causing connectivity issues and impeding productivity. It's essential to identify and fix NIC issues quickly and methodically to restore flawless network functionality, including inspecting physical connections and updating drivers.

9.2.3 Wiring and hardware issues.

Assume you are a homeowner and your living room is equipped with a home theater system. To create an immersive entertainment experience, you have a high-definition television, surround sound, a game console, and a media streaming device all connected. You've observed, though, that recently the audio and video quality aren't as clear as they once were, and occasionally the sound even totally stops.

You start to investigate the problem. When you first examine all of your device connections, you discover that the HDMI cable that connects your gaming console to the television has a little amount of fraying and is slightly bent at one end. In the hopes that it was the cause of the issue, you straighten it up and secure the connection. But even after doing this, the problems still exist.

You then look at the audio setup. You see that the speaker wires are twisted and some are even exposed near the ends of the speakers that are linked to your surround sound system. You carefully arrange the wires to avoid any contact with one another and make sure they are all fully put into the receiver because you think this might be the issue.

Your efforts haven't changed the audio or video issues. You decide to investigate the hardware issue further out of frustration. You check the internal components of the media streaming device and the game console by opening them up. Upon additional study, you discover that the gaming console's cooling fan isn't operating correctly. This might be causing the console to overheat, which would impair its functionality and perhaps be the cause of the audio and video problems.

You need to remove any dust or debris that might be obstructing the cooling fan's operation to solve the issue. Additionally, make sure that the device's internal temperature sensors are working properly. When you turn on the gaming system after doing this, the audio and video quality are once again at their best.

In this case, your home entertainment system's performance was being hampered by a confluence of wiring and hardware problems. The audio and video issues you were having were caused by a frayed cable, twisted wiring, and a broken cooling fan. You were able to improve the caliber of your entertainment setup by methodically identifying and resolving each of these problems. This situation demonstrates how crucial it is to examine hardware elements as well as physical connections while addressing technical issues.

9.3: DHCP (Dynamic Host Configuration Protocol)

Troubleshooting DHCP (Dynamic Host Configuration Protocol) entails locating and fixing problems with the automatic assignment of IP addresses and network configuration to devices. Checking the availability of the DHCP server, confirming its configuration settings, and making sure that the network equipment, such as routers and switches, is operating properly are standard procedures used when encountering issues. Furthermore, it is crucial to look at client-side settings, such as the network adapter's setup and any firewalls. Analysis of the DHCP logs can reveal important information about problems or conflicts. Administrators can identify and fix DHCP-related problems by methodically looking at these areas, providing effective network connectivity and communication.

9.3.1: DHCP server failures

Consider a situation where PCs on a company network are set up so that a DHCP server will automatically assign IP addresses to employees' computers. One day, staff members began to complain about connectivity problems and certain machines becoming unable to access the network resources.

The network administrator discovers after some inquiry that the
The DHCP server has failed. The following could be the causes of the
failure:

1. Server Hardware Failure: It's possible that the server's
    hardware, like the hard disk or network interface card, has
    a fault and cannot reply to DHCP queries.
2. IP Address Exhaustion: The DHCP server may run out of
    IP addresses to assign. This might happen if there's
    an unanticipated inflow of new devices or if the address pool
    has a small range of IP address assignments.
3. Configuration Issues: Failures could be caused by an
    incorrect configuration of the DHCP server parameters.
    For instance, clients could overburden the server if the
    DHCP lease period is set too low and they regularly request
    new addresses.
4. Network Connectivity: Clients may be unable to reach the
    DHCP server if it is located on a different subnet or VLAN due
    to network configuration errors or routing problems.

The administrator could take the following actions to resolve this
situation:

1. Hardware Check: Check the hardware condition of the server
    to make sure every part is operating properly.
2. IP Address Management: Increase the capacity of the
    DHCP address pool to support more devices, or use

DHCP reservations for essential devices to guarantee they always get the same IP address.

3. Configuration Review: Check the configuration settings for the DHCP server to make sure that lease lengths, IP ranges, and other parameters are configured correctly.

4. Network Analysis: Verify the network architecture to make sure that all necessary subnets or VLANs may connect to the DHCP server.

5. Firewall Inspection: Check the firewall settings on the DHCP server to ensure they are not preventing incoming DHCP traffic.

The network administrator can restore connectivity for the impacted devices and guarantee steady network operations by quickly diagnosing and fixing DHCP server issues.

9.3.2: IP address lease problems

Imagine a medium-sized organization where several workers have their computers connected to the company network. To automatically assign IP addresses to the devices, the office utilizes a DHCP server. However, some staff members occasionally have connectivity problems.

The network administrator conducts further research and finds that the DHCP server is assigning IP addresses with extremely little lease lengths, such as 10 minutes. As a result, devices must frequently renew their IP addresses, which could cause network connectivity issues.

The short lease duration in this situation is the IP address lease dilemma. This could lead to the following number of problems:

1. Frequent Address Renewal: Devices' frequent IP lease

renewal uses up network resources and places a burden on both clients and servers

2. Connectivity Interruptions: An IP address can be transferred to another device if a device doesn't renew its lease promptly. The original device may lose network connectivity as a result, disrupting ongoing tasks.

3. DHCP Server Overload: Numerous lease renewal requests are placed on the DHCP server, which could hinder its performance and responsiveness.

4. Network Congestion: The ongoing renewal procedure may result in an increase in DHCP-related network traffic, which could impede overall network performance and cause congestion.

To address this issue, the network administrator could take the following steps:

1. Lease Duration Adjustment: Depending on the needs of the network, extend the lease period to a more suitable amount of time, such as a few hours or days. As a result, lease renewals happen less frequently.

2. Monitoring and Analysis: To determine which devices are regularly asking for new leases and to examine the trend of lease renewals, keep an eye on the DHCP server logs.

3. DHCP Reservation: For crucial hardware, such as printers,

servers, and network devices, implement DHCP reservations. Because of this, there is no need to frequently renew the lease on these devices because they will always receive the same IP address.

4. Address Pool Sizing: Make sure that the DHCP address pool is big enough to handle the amount of networked devices. Devices may struggle to find an open IP address if the pool is too limited.

5. Testing and Communication: After changing the lease's duration, let the staff know about the change and urge them to let you know if they continue to experience connectivity problems so that you can investigate them further.

The network administrator can improve network stability, lower DHCP server load, and offer a better experience for all connected devices by fixing IP address lease issues and optimizing lease durations.

9.4: Routing and Default Gateway Problem

This issue relates to the difficulty of successfully managing network traffic inside a computer network. Routing includes figuring out the best route for data packets to go across numerous interconnected devices from the source to the destination. In this procedure, the default gateway is essential because it acts as the point at which traffic leaves the local network to travel to locations outside of it. Routing problems and incorrect default gateway setup can cause communication breakdowns, as data fails to reach its target location or travels down inefficient channels, causing delays or even transmission failures. To ensure seamless and effective data flow across the network, the solutions to these issues necessitate a firm grasp of network topology, adequate routing table configuration, and precise default gateway settings.

9.4.1 Incorrect routing table entries

Let's explore the idea of "Incorrect routing table entries" in more detail using a real-world illustration of a home network with several devices connected to the router.

Imagine that your home network consists of a router and several devices. You possess a printer, a smart TV, and Computer X. The traffic between these gadgets and the internet is controlled by the router. The routing table of the router serves as a guide for how each device should send and receive data.

You choose to configure a Virtual Private Network (VPN) on Computer X to increase your online security. On Computer X, you unintentionally change the routing table when configuring the VPN.

You unintentionally modify the entire routing table with the VPN settings instead of only adding a specific route for the VPN traffic. The necessary routes for global internet access or local network communication are consequently no longer included in Computer X's routing table. All traffic is routed exclusively through the VPN tunnel on these routes.

As a result of the wrong routing table entry, the following occurs:

1. Local Network Communication Disruption: The printer and smart TV are two examples of gadgets on your home network that Computer X can no longer communicate with. Because Computer

X is unable to figure out how to send the data to these devices, attempts to exchange files or print documents are unsuccessful.

2. Internet Connectivity Issues: Computer X can access the internet through the VPN tunnel, but because of the additional encryption and routing, the connection is slower. Additionally, because they are ignorant of the new routing path, other networked devices like printers and smart TVs are unable to access the internet.

3. VPN Isolation: Computer X is virtually cut off from the local network while the VPN is in use. In some security settings, this might be desired, but in this instance, it's an unintentional effect.

To fix the problem:

The routing table on Computer X has to be fixed. You should keep the current routes for local network connectivity and public internet access while adding particular routes for VPN traffic. This guarantees that each sort of traffic is pointed in the right direction.

In conclusion, erroneous routing table entries can result in network seclusion, local communication disruptions, and issues with internet connectivity. It emphasizes how crucial it is to correctly configure routing tables to guarantee smooth data transfer between devices on both local and wide-area networks.

9.4.2 Router and switch failures affecting routing

"Router and switch failures affecting routing" refers to a situation in which faults or failures in networking equipment, such as routers and switches, can cause interruptions in the routing process, resulting in communication problems within a network. Let's investigate this idea with an in-depth illustration:

Think of yourself as the network administrator of a sizable office with a router, several switches, and numerous computers. Traffic between the internal network of your office and the public internet is managed by the router. To provide effective data exchange, the switches help link various office equipment.

Let's assume that one of the switches experiences a hardware issue and ceases to operate correctly. As a result of this:

1. Isolated Devices: Devices connected to the failed switch might become isolated from the rest of the network. For instance, if Computer X and Computer Y are connected to the same switch and the switch fails, Computer X won't be able to communicate with Computer Y, even though they are physically close to each other.

2. Network Segment Isolation: Two network segments may become isolated from one another if the failed switch serves as a bridge connecting them. There won't be any communication between devices in one segment and those in the other segment. Processes at work that depend on inter-segment communication could be significantly disrupted by this.

3. Routing Disruptions: In more complicated circumstances, if the failed switch was routing traffic in a certain method, its failure could stop the routing procedure altogether. For instance, if the switch was in charge of routing traffic from a particular

department to the router for internet access, the malfunction might cause that department to lose internet connectivity.

4. Redundancy and Failover: Redundancy and failover methods are frequently used in high-end networking installations to reduce these problems. A backup device seamlessly assumes control if one router or switch fails, ensuring uninterrupted network operation. Failures can still have a big impact if these procedures are not set up or handled correctly, though.

To solve these issues:

1. Replace or Repair: To get the network back to working normally, the broken switch needs to be replaced or fixed. This can entail bringing in backup tools, getting in touch with technical help, or, if feasible, doing repairs.

2. Network Redesign: In some circumstances, network redesign may be required to stop future failures from creating significant outages. The resilience of the network can be increased through redundancy, load balancing, and appropriate segment isolation techniques.

3. Monitoring and Maintenance: Networking hardware should be regularly inspected and maintained to assist in spotting possible problems before they become complete failures. This includes verifying the efficiency of the hardware, upgrading the firmware, and ensuring enough ventilation and electricity.

In essence, network communication and routing can be negatively impacted by router and switch failures. It emphasizes how crucial dependable hardware, successful redundancy plans, and proactive maintenance are in ensuring a network's stability and availability.

9.5 Packet Capturing, Analysis and Wireshark

The act of intercepting and capturing data packets as they go through a network is known as packet capturing. The packets' contents can subsequently be examined to comprehend various facets of network behavior using this acquired data. This includes figuring out connectivity problems, spotting malicious activity, improving network performance, and making sure that all applications and services are running properly.

The process of packet analysis is looking at the individual data packets that go through computer networks. It's a fundamental method for identifying and resolving network problems. The popular packet analysis tool Wireshark enables users to record, examine, and decipher the information moving between devices on a network. Users can examine packet contents with Wireshark, find the causes of network congestion, find the exact location of communication problems, and learn more about how networks behave. This application gives a visual representation of data traffic, assisting IT workers in comprehending how data moves through a network and assisting them in resolving connectivity, security, and performance-related issues.

9.5.1 Using Wireshark for Troubleshooting

Using Wireshark for troubleshooting is a highly effective method for locating and fixing network-related problems. Network administrators and analysts can capture and examine packets using Wireshark, which enables them to find the source of issues and improve network performance.

Here is an illustration of how to use Wireshark for troubleshooting:

Case Study: Slow Website Loading

Imagine that a company's employees are less productive because websites take too long to load. The IT team chose to look at the problem using Wireshark.

1. Packet Capture: On the network interface connected to the troubled users, the IT team starts a packet capture. Every packet that passes over that interface is captured by Wireshark.

2. Filtering: The team uses a filter to display only HTTP and HTTPS packets so that they may concentrate on web traffic. This focuses on the data that was obtained on the pertinent traffic.

3. Analysis: The team examines the packets and finds that the response times between the client's browser requests and the server responses are excessively long. In addition, they see several retransmissions and out-of-order packets.

4. Latency Issue: This pattern suggests a latency issue, which may be brought on by network congestion or communication mistakes. When the team discovers numerous TCP retransmissions, which would indicate that some packets were lost and needed to be retransmitted, their assumption that some packets were lost is confirmed.

5. Root Cause Identification: Further investigation reveals that a network switch close to the section of customers that is having

problems is occasionally overloaded, resulting in packet failures and retransmissions. The sluggish loading of the webpage is being caused by this switch's inefficiency.

Resolution: The IT team chooses to replace the network switch with a more capable one to fix the problem. With this upgrade, network congestion is lessened, packet loss is decreased, and overall network performance is enhanced.

In this instance, Wireshark assisted the IT team in identifying the precise reason why the webpages were loading slowly, which was a clogged switch that was causing packet loss and retransmissions. It would have been much harder to diagnose this issue without Wireshark's comprehensive packet-level insights.

Network experts get a detailed view of network traffic thanks to Wireshark's ability to capture and analyze packets, which enables them to investigate and solve problems quickly. Wireshark is still a crucial tool for troubleshooting complicated networking systems, whether it's for diagnosing latency, discovering unauthorized network activity, or optimizing network configurations.

9.5.2 Analyzing network traffic to identify issues

Maintaining a dependable and secure network environment necessitates the practice of analyzing network traffic to spot problems. Network administrators can find abnormalities, identify issues, and fix them by carefully studying the data packet flow.

Here is an illustration of how network traffic analysis can be used to locate and fix a problem:

Case Study: DDoS Attack Detection

Consider a scenario where a small e-commerce website suddenly becomes slow and unresponsive. The IT department believes that the website's server is being overloaded by a significant amount of malicious traffic or a Distributed Denial of Service (DDoS) attack.

1. Traffic Analysis: The IT staff uses a network analysis tool to track the patterns of incoming traffic. They can distinguish between legitimate user requests and possibly harmful communications by examining the network flow.

2. Traffic Spike Identification: The team notices an unusual increase in inbound requests that is far higher than the typical traffic to the website. Because all of these requests are focused on a small number of URLs, there is significant congestion.

3. Source Identification: The team discovers a high number of requests coming from various areas but with similar features, including recurrent patterns in the data payload, by looking at the source IP addresses of the incoming requests.

4. Signature Matching: The team compares known DDoS attack signatures with the traffic patterns and features. Based on the investigation, a DDoS attack is being launched against the website.

5. Mitigation: With this knowledge, the IT staff proceeds to mitigate the assault right away. To stop or lessen the effects of the malicious traffic, they use network security techniques like

rate limitation or traffic filtering.

6. Monitoring and Prevention: The IT team kept track of network traffic after successfully neutralizing the attack to look for any odd patterns. To stop future DDoS assaults from crashing the website, they also put extra security measures in place, such as setting up a Web Application Firewall (WAF) or using content delivery networks (CDNs).

In this case, the IT team's quick detection and mitigation of a DDoS attack on the e-commerce website were made possible by network traffic analysis. The team was able to locate the source of the performance problem and take quick measures to secure the network by carefully studying the flow of data packets and spotting odd patterns.

Understanding traffic patterns, protocols, and potential dangers requires more than just simple monitoring of network traffic. In the connected digital environment of today, this approach is essential for ensuring the integrity, availability, and security of networks.

9.6 Tools and Utilities for Troubleshooting

Tools and utilities for troubleshooting are crucial resources that help IT specialists locate, recognize, and fix a variety of problems in computer networks and systems. These tools cover a wide range of uses, from command-line utilities like "ping" and "traceroute" that help evaluate network connectivity and identify latency issues to packet analyzers like Wireshark that probe into network data. Finding system faults and anomalies is made easier with the use of diagnostic tools like "Event Viewer" on Windows and "Syslog" on Linux. Security threats are countered by antivirus and anti-malware software, while resource use is analyzed by performance monitoring programs like "Task Manager" and "top". Together, these tools equip IT staff to quickly resolve technical issues and maintain the efficiency of digital infrastructures.

9.6.1 Ping and traceroute commands

The "ping" and "traceroute" commands are basic networking tools used to identify network connectivity problems and track the route taken by data packets as they cross the internet or a local network. Let's examine these commands in greater depth with an illustration:

Ping Command

A target IP address or hostname receives a string of ICMP (Internet Control Message Protocol) echo request packets when you issue the "ping" command. It calculates the time it takes for packets to travel from their source to their destination and back, which aids in determining how responsive the target host is.

Illustration

C:\Users\KM-PC>ping www.google.com

Pinging www.google.com [216.58.205.36] with 32 bytes of data:
Reply from 216.58.205.36: bytes=32 time=143ms TTL=114
Reply from 216.58.205.36: bytes=32 time=166ms TTL=114
Reply from 216.58.205.36: bytes=32 time=203ms TTL=114
Reply from 216.58.205.36: bytes=32 time=290ms TTL=114

Ping statistics for 216.58.205.36:
    Packets: Sent = 4, Received = 4, Lost = 0 (0% loss),
Approximate round trip times in milli-seconds:
    Minimum = 143ms, Maximum = 290ms, Average = 200ms

The command in this illustration sends ICMP echo requests to the servers of Google. The result shows the round-trip time (in milliseconds) for each packet, which represents the amount of time it takes for a packet to leave the client and return to Google's servers. This data may show instances of packet loss, network latency problems, or unresponsive hosts.

Traceroute Command

On Windows and Unix-like operating systems (including Linux and macOS), the "tracert" and "traceroute" utilities, respectively, are command-line tools used to send packets with increasing Time-To-Live (TTL) values to track the path that data packets traverse from their source to their destination. As the TTL decreases across each intermediate router, the router sends an ICMP Time Exceeded message back to the source when the TTL approaches zero. This enables the source to determine the packets' route.

Illustration

```
Microsoft Windows [Version 10.0.19045.4412]
(c) Microsoft Corporation. All rights reserved.


C:\Users\KM-PC>tracert www.google.com


Tracing route to www.google.com [216.58.205.36]
over a maximum of 30 hops:

 1   236 ms     3 ms     3 ms  192.168.0.1
 2    41 ms    37 ms    27 ms  10.0.3.78
 3     *         *         *     Request timed out.
 4    42 ms    20 ms    25 ms  197.232.61.186
 5    49 ms    19 ms    19 ms  41.215.131.26
 6     *         *       66 ms  41.222.9.86
 7    26 ms    31 ms    31 ms  72.14.205.58
 8    26 ms    25 ms    47 ms  172.253.53.51
 9   147 ms   203 ms   306 ms  142.251.51.165
10   198 ms   197 ms   150 ms  108.170.255.211
11   136 ms   139 ms   151 ms  172.253.73.61
12   159 ms   158 ms   179 ms  mil04s24-in-f4.1e100.net [216.58.205.36]

Trace complete.
```

When the command is used, a list of the routers that are found on the route that the packets follow to go to their destination is shown. It aids in locating potential bottlenecks, network congestion, and routing problems by displaying the IP addresses and round-trip timings for each hop.

Illustration II

Let's say your internet connection is unreliable. The "ping" command can be used to assess a server's responsiveness, such as Google's DNS server (8.8.8.8).

```
C:\Users\KM-PC>ping 8.8.8.8

Pinging 8.8.8.8 with 32 bytes of data:
Reply from 8.8.8.8: bytes=32 time=26ms TTL=115
Reply from 8.8.8.8: bytes=32 time=37ms TTL=115
Reply from 8.8.8.8: bytes=32 time=37ms TTL=115
Reply from 8.8.8.8: bytes=32 time=40ms TTL=115

Ping statistics for 8.8.8.8:
    Packets: Sent = 4, Received = 4, Lost = 0 (0% loss),
Approximate round trip times in milli-seconds:
    Minimum = 26ms, Maximum = 40ms, Average = 35ms
```

When packet loss or extremely long ping times occur, you can use the "tracert/traceroute" command to find the server's route:

```
C:\Users\KM-PC>tracert 8.8.8.8

Tracing route to dns.google [8.8.8.8]
over a maximum of 30 hops:

1    3 ms    2 ms    6 ms  192.168.0.1
2   42 ms   49 ms   45 ms  10.0.3.78
3    *       *       *      Request timed out.
4   37 ms   42 ms   31 ms  197.232.61.186
5   43 ms   19 ms   47 ms  41.215.131.26
6    *       *       *      Request timed out.
7   51 ms  325 ms   37 ms  72.14.205.58
8   49 ms   26 ms   47 ms  108.170.253.145
9   50 ms   49 ms   51 ms  72.14.238.159
10  41 ms   31 ms   32 ms  dns.google [8.8.8.8]

Trace complete.
```

You can spot where there are delays or connectivity problems by looking at the traceroute report. If there is a noticeable delay at a certain hop, there may be an issue with that router or its network connection.

The "ping" and "traceroute" programs are helpful resources for identifying network connectivity issues and figuring out the route that data packets take over a network, in short. For network administrators and anybody solving network-related difficulties, they are crucial utilities.

9.6.2 ipconfig and ifconfig utilities

On Windows and Unix-like operating systems (including Linux and macOS), the "ipconfig" and "ifconfig" utilities, respectively, are command-line tools used to manage and display network configuration data. These tools offer crucial information on network interfaces, IP addresses, subnet masks, and other topics.

Let's explore each usefulness with an illustration:

ipconfig (Windows)

Windows operating systems use the "ipconfig" program to examine and alter network setup settings. It offers details on the IP configuration of the local computer, such as IP addresses, subnet masks and default gateways.

```
C:\>ipconfig/all

Windows IP Configuration

    Host Name . . . . . . . . . . . : DESKTOP-BBF5MQ0
    Primary Dns Suffix  . . . . . . :
    Node Type . . . . . . . . . . . : Hybrid
    IP Routing Enabled. . . . . . . : No
    WINS Proxy Enabled. . . . . . . : No

Ethernet adapter Ethernet:

    Media State . . . . . . . . . . : Media disconnected
    Connection-specific DNS Suffix  . :
    Description . . . . . . . . . . : Realtek PCIe GBE Family Controller
    Physical Address. . . . . . . . : 8C-DC-D4-CC-C7-8B
    DHCP Enabled. . . . . . . . . . : Yes
    Autoconfiguration Enabled . . . . : Yes

Ethernet adapter Ethernet 4:

    Connection-specific DNS Suffix  . :
    Description . . . . . . . . . . : VirtualBox Host-Only Ethernet Adapter
    Physical Address. . . . . . . . : 0A-00-27-00-00-09
    DHCP Enabled. . . . . . . . . . : No
    Autoconfiguration Enabled . . . . : Yes
    Link-local IPv6 Address . . . . . : fe80::fcc7:248e:b0d:70dd%9(Preferred)
    IPv4 Address. . . . . . . . . . : 192.168.56.1(Preferred)
    Subnet Mask . . . . . . . . . . : 255.255.255.0
    Default Gateway . . . . . . . . :
    DHCPv6 IAID . . . . . . . . . . : 856293415
    DHCPv6 Client DUID. . . . . . . : 00-01-00-01-2B-5E-30-F9-8C-DC-D4-CC-C7-8B
    DNS Servers . . . . . . . . . . : fec0:0:0:ffff::1%1
                                      fec0:0:0:ffff::2%1
                                      fec0:0:0:ffff::3%1
    NetBIOS over Tcpip. . . . . . . : Enabled
```

Wireless LAN adapter Local Area Connection* 3:

   Media State . . . . : Media disconnected
   Connection-specific DNS Suffix . :
   Description . . . . : Microsoft Wi-Fi Direct Virtual Adapter #2
   Physical Address. . . . . : D8-FC-93-0A-55-BA
   DHCP Enabled. . . . . : Yes
   Autoconfiguration Enabled . . . . : Yes

Wireless LAN adapter Local Area Connection* 4:

   Media State . . . . : Media disconnected
   Connection-specific DNS Suffix . :
   Description . . . . : Microsoft Wi-Fi Direct Virtual Adapter #3
   Physical Address. . . . . : DA-FC-93-0A-55-B9
   DHCP Enabled. . . . . : Yes
   Autoconfiguration Enabled . . . . : Yes

Wireless LAN adapter Wi-Fi:

   Connection-specific DNS Suffix . :
   Description . . . . : Intel(R) Dual Band Wireless-N 7260
   Physical Address. . . . . : D8-FC-93-0A-55-B9
   DHCP Enabled. . . . . : Yes
   Autoconfiguration Enabled . . . . : Yes
   Link-local IPv6 Address . . . . . : fe80::5171:adb:1e29:82f8%23(Preferred)
   IPv4 Address. . . . . : 192.168.0.110(Preferred)
   Subnet Mask . . . . : 255.255.255.0
   Lease Obtained. . . . . : Saturday, May 18, 2024 4:45:35 PM
   Lease Expires . . . . : Sunday, May 19, 2024 4:48:38 PM
   Default Gateway . . . . : 192.168.0.1
   DHCP Server . . . . : 192.168.0.1
   DHCPv6 IAID . . . . : 98106515
   DHCPv6 Client DUID. . . . . : 00-01-00-01-2B-5E-30-F9-8C-DC-D4-CC-C7-8B
   DNS Servers . . . . : 192.168.0.1
   NetBIOS over Tcpip. . . . . : Enabled

This command will show detailed network data for all of the computer's active network interfaces when entered into the Windows command prompt. It contains information such as the IP address, subnet mask, default gateway, and addresses for the DHCP server and DNS servers. Using this knowledge can help you identify connectivity problems, confirm IP setups, and make sure your network settings are correct.

ifconfig (Unix-like systems)

In Unix-like operating systems (such as Linux, macOS, etc.), the "ifconfig" utility is used to configure and display data about network interfaces. It can be used to distribute IP addresses, enable or disable interfaces, and compile data about the network.

```
$ ifconfig
eth0: flags=4163<UP,BROADCAST,RUNNING,MULTICAST>  mtu 1500
        inet 192.168.0.109  netmask 255.255.255.0  broadcast 192.168.0.255
        inet6 fe80::a00:27ff:fefb:6e9  prefixlen 64  scopeid 0x20<link>
        ether 08:00:27:fb:06:e9  txqueuelen 1000  (Ethernet)
        RX packets 76  bytes 28132 (27.4 KiB)
        RX errors 0  dropped 0  overruns 0  frame 0
        TX packets 62  bytes 21398 (20.8 KiB)
        TX errors 0  dropped 0 overruns 0  carrier 0  collisions 0

lo: flags=73<UP,LOOPBACK,RUNNING>  mtu 65536
        inet 127.0.0.1  netmask 255.0.0.0
        inet6 ::1  prefixlen 128  scopeid 0x10<host>
        loop  txqueuelen 1000  (Local Loopback)
        RX packets 24  bytes 1440 (1.4 KiB)
        RX errors 0  dropped 0  overruns 0  frame 0
        TX packets 24  bytes 1440 (1.4 KiB)
        TX errors 0  dropped 0 overruns 0  carrier 0  collisions 0
```

This command displays comprehensive details about the network interface when used on a Linux system. The interface's IP address, subnet mask, hardware address (MAC address), and other pertinent configuration information are all included in the output.

The commands "ipconfig" and "ifconfig" are both crucial resources for users and network administrators debugging network-related issues. They make it simpler to detect and fix connectivity issues, modify network settings, and guarantee smooth communication inside a network by giving instant access to crucial networking information.

9.6.3 netstat utility

A command-line tool called netstat (network statistics) is used to show different network-related data on a computer system. Network connections, routing tables, and interface statistics are some of the information covered in detail. It is particularly beneficial for evaluating network connections, monitoring network activity, and spotting network-related issues.

Most Unix-like operating systems, including Linux and macOS, can also use the netstat tool. The nestat command utility has been deprecated in favor of newer utilities like ss (socket statistics) and ip commands to provide better performance and functionality.

The syntax for netstat command is as follows:

netstat [options]

Here are a few typical Netstat options:

-t: View TCP connections.

-u: View UDP connections.

-n: Display numeric addresses rather than trying to resolve hostnames.

-a: All connections, both listening and not listening, should be displayed.

-p: Display the connection's owner process for each.

-r: Display the routing table for the kernel.

-s: Display data about various network protocol statistics.

Here's an illustration of how the netstat command could be used to show active TCP connections:

```
Microsoft Windows [Version 10.0.19045.4412]
(c) Microsoft Corporation. All rights reserved.

C:\Users\KM-PC>netstat -a

Active Connections

  Proto  Local Address          Foreign Address        State
  TCP    0.0.0.0:135            DESKTOP-BBF5MQ0:0      LISTENING
  TCP    0.0.0.0:445            DESKTOP-BBF5MQ0:0      LISTENING
  TCP    0.0.0.0:3389           DESKTOP-BBF5MQ0:0      LISTENING
  TCP    0.0.0.0:5040           DESKTOP-BBF5MQ0:0      LISTENING
  TCP    0.0.0.0:5357           DESKTOP-BBF5MQ0:0      LISTENING
  TCP    0.0.0.0:7070           DESKTOP-BBF5MQ0:0      LISTENING
  TCP    0.0.0.0:11685          DESKTOP-BBF5MQ0:0      LISTENING
  TCP    0.0.0.0:49664          DESKTOP-BBF5MQ0:0      LISTENING
  TCP    0.0.0.0:49665          DESKTOP-BBF5MQ0:0      LISTENING
  TCP    0.0.0.0:49666          DESKTOP-BBF5MQ0:0      LISTENING
  TCP    0.0.0.0:49667          DESKTOP-BBF5MQ0:0      LISTENING
  TCP    0.0.0.0:49668          DESKTOP-BBF5MQ0:0      LISTENING
  TCP    0.0.0.0:49669          DESKTOP-BBF5MQ0:0      LISTENING
  TCP    0.0.0.0:49674          DESKTOP-BBF5MQ0:0      LISTENING
  TCP    127.0.0.1:45780        DESKTOP-BBF5MQ0:59887  ESTABLISHED
  TCP    127.0.0.1:51495        DESKTOP-BBF5MQ0:0      LISTENING
  TCP    127.0.0.1:59882        DESKTOP-BBF5MQ0:0      LISTENING
  TCP    127.0.0.1:59887        DESKTOP-BBF5MQ0:45780  ESTABLISHED
  TCP    127.0.0.1:59899        DESKTOP-BBF5MQ0:59900  ESTABLISHED
  TCP    127.0.0.1:59900        DESKTOP-BBF5MQ0:59899  ESTABLISHED
  TCP    127.0.0.1:59901        DESKTOP-BBF5MQ0:59902  ESTABLISHED
  TCP    127.0.0.1:59902        DESKTOP-BBF5MQ0:59901  ESTABLISHED
  TCP    127.0.0.1:59903        DESKTOP-BBF5MQ0:59904  ESTABLISHED
  TCP    127.0.0.1:59904        DESKTOP-BBF5MQ0:59903  ESTABLISHED
  TCP    127.0.0.1:59905        DESKTOP-BBF5MQ0:59906  ESTABLISHED
  TCP    127.0.0.1:59906        DESKTOP-BBF5MQ0:59905  ESTABLISHED
  TCP    127.0.0.1:59907        DESKTOP-BBF5MQ0:59908  ESTABLISHED
  TCP    127.0.0.1:59908        DESKTOP-BBF5MQ0:59907  ESTABLISHED
  TCP    127.0.0.1:59909        DESKTOP-BBF5MQ0:59910  ESTABLISHED
  TCP    127.0.0.1:59910        DESKTOP-BBF5MQ0:59909  ESTABLISHED
  TCP    192.168.0.110:139      DESKTOP-BBF5MQ0:0      LISTENING
```

```
UDP    0.0.0.0:50001              *:*
UDP    0.0.0.0:55020              *:*
UDP    127.0.0.1:1900             *:*
UDP    127.0.0.1:6771             *:*
UDP    127.0.0.1:52396            *:*
UDP    127.0.0.1:63808            *:*
UDP    127.0.0.1:63907            *:*
UDP    192.168.0.110:137          *:*
UDP    192.168.0.110:138          *:*
UDP    192.168.0.110:1900         *:*
UDP    192.168.0.110:6771         *:*
UDP    192.168.0.110:63807        *:*
UDP    192.168.0.110:63906        *:*
UDP    192.168.56.1:137           *:*
UDP    192.168.56.1:138           *:*
UDP    192.168.56.1:1900          *:*
UDP    192.168.56.1:6771          *:*
UDP    192.168.56.1:63806         *:*
UDP    192.168.56.1:63905         *:*
UDP    [::]:500                   *:*
UDP    [::]:3389                  *:*
UDP    [::]:3702                  *:*
UDP    [::]:3702                  *:*
UDP    [::]:4500                  *:*
UDP    [::]:5353                  *:*
UDP    [::]:5353                  *:*
UDP    [::]:5353                  *:*
UDP    [::]:5353                  *:*
UDP    [::]:5353                  *:*
UDP    [::]:5355                  *:*
UDP    [::]:11685                 *:*
UDP    [::]:55021                 *:*
UDP    [::1]:1900                 *:*
UDP    [::1]:58295                *:*
UDP    [::1]:63904                *:*
UDP    [fe80::5171:adb:1e29:82f8%23]:1900   *:*
UDP    [fe80::5171:adb:1e29:82f8%23]:63903  *:*
UDP    [fe80::fcc7:248e:b0d:70dd%9]:1900    *:*
UDP    [fe80::fcc7:248e:b0d:70dd%9]:63902   *:*
```

Keep in mind that depending on your operating system and the installed version of the tool, the netstat command's precise output and available options may change. For detailed information on your system, it's always a good idea to refer to the manual (man netstat) or help (netstat --help).

9.6.4 nslookup utility

The command-line program nslookup (short for "name server lookup") is used to query DNS servers to learn about domain names, IP addresses, and other DNS-related information. It is a helpful tool for diagnosing DNS-related difficulties, checking DNS records, and resolving network issues with domain names.

Linux, macOS, and Windows are among the numerous Unix-like operating systems that support nslookup. It's important to keep in mind, though, that certain operating systems, namely Unix-like operating systems, have begun to replace nslookup with alternative utilities like dig or host for more sophisticated DNS searching capabilities.

The syntax for nslookup command is as follows:

nslookup [options] [hostname]

Here are a few typical nslookup options:

-query=<type>: Indicates the kind of DNS record to look for (such as A, MX, NS, etc.).

-server=<server>: the DNS server that will be used for the query is specified.

-type=<type>: Indicates the kind of DNS record to look for (the same as -query).

```
C:\>nslookup google.com
Server:  UnKnown
Address:  192.168.0.1

Non-authoritative answer:
Name:   google.com
Addresses:  2a00:1450:4002:411::200e
       142.251.209.46
```

The IP addresses linked to the domain, the default DNS server in use, and other DNS-related information will be displayed.

Depending on the version of the program installed and the operating system you are running, the nslookup command's precise behavior and options may change.

9.6.5 Network diagnostic tools for different operating systems

These are just a few illustrations of the various operating system-specific network diagnostic tools that are available. The tool you choose will rely on the particular problem you're trying to diagnose as well as the features each tool has to offer. For the most recent information on how to use these tools efficiently, it is advised to go to the documentation for each tool and to check up-to-date resources.

The few often employed network diagnostic tools for various operating systems is as follows:

1. **Linux**

    a. ping: An easy-to-use tool for sending ICMP echo queries to hosts to test network connectivity.

    b. traceroute or traceroute6: Displays the path that packets travel to get to their destination, which is useful for figuring out network hops and latency.

    c. netstat or ss: Show network statistics, such as connections that are active, listening ports, and routing details.

    d. ifconfig or ip: Sets up and shows routing tables, IP addresses, and information about network interfaces.

    e. dig: assists in troubleshooting DNS-related problems, and query DNS servers for various DNS records.

2. **Windows**

    a. **ping:** The ICMP echo requests used to test network connectivity are the same as in the Linux version.

    b. **tracert:** Similar to Linux's traceroute command, which shows the route to a particular location.

    c. **ipconfig:** Displays IP setup, including gateway data, subnet masks, and IP addresses.

    d. **netstat:** Displays information about ports, routing, and active network connections.

    e. **nslookup:** Obtain DNS records by asking DNS servers.

    f. **PathPing:** provides more thorough information about network performance throughout the path by combining the characteristics of ping and tracert.

3. **macOS**

   a. **ping:** It uses ICMP echo requests to evaluate network connectivity, much like in Linux and Windows.

   b. **traceroute:** An integrated version of traceroute is available in macOS for network path analysis.

   c. **ifconfig or ip:** Displays IP setup, including gateway data, subnet masks, and IP addresses.

   d. **netstat or ss:** Display network connections and statistics.

   e. **nslookup:** Request DNS records from the DNS servers.

   f. **Network Utility:** a graphical application for macOS that offers ping, traceroute, whois, and port scanning among other network diagnostic tools.

4. **BSD**

   Ping, traceroute, netstat, and nslookup are among the utilities that BSD-based systems frequently share with Linux or macOS.

   Network interfaces and IP configuration are managed using ifconfig or ip.

   Instead of nslookup, some BSD systems may utilize host to perform DNS searches.

5. **Network-Specific Tools**

   a) **Wireshark:** A multiplatform packet analyzer that records and examines network data down to the packet level.

   b) **Nmap:** An effective open-source program for port scanning and security audits of networks.

c) **Tcpdump:** A network traffic capture and analysis command-line packet analyzer accessible on Unix-like computers.

9.7 IPv4 Security Considerations

IPv4 network security requires tackling a variety of attacks and vulnerabilities. To protect against unauthorized access and harmful activities, it is common practice to build tight access restrictions, firewall rules, and intrusion detection systems. Sensitive data can also be protected while in transit via encryption techniques, and frequent vulnerability assessments and patch management can help reduce any dangers brought on by software flaws. A thorough security plan for IPv4 networks should involve ongoing monitoring, quick incident response, and a proactive strategy for reducing potential threats.

9.7.1: Identifying security vulnerabilities in IPv4 networks

Maintaining network security requires constantly looking for security flaws in IPv4 networks. Numerous vulnerabilities can be exploited by hostile actors on IPv4 networks to obtain unauthorized access, stop services, or compromise important data. Here is a description of the procedure and an illustration:

Identifying Vulnerabilities Process:

1. **Network Discovery:** List every system and device that is joined to the network. Utilize devices like network scanners and discovery tools to compile a list of all currently active IP addresses, hardware, and software.

2. **Vulnerability Scanning:** Use vulnerability scanning tools to find software and networked devices that have known security flaws. The system versions and configurations that these programs test against a database of known vulnerabilities.

3. **Penetration Testing:** To simulate attacks and find potential entry holes for attackers, conduct ethical hacking exercises. Penetration testing aids in finding vulnerabilities that automated methods might miss.

4. **Patch and Update Management:** Apply security updates and fixes to systems, programs, and gadgets regularly. Vendors frequently find and patch vulnerabilities, so it's important to stay current.

5. **Security Configurations:** To make sure they are properly set up to prevent unwanted access, network devices, firewalls, and routers should have their security configurations reviewed and modified.

6. **Monitoring and Intrusion Detection:** Utilize intrusion detection and network monitoring tools to spot shady activities and potential security breaches.

Illustration:

Let's look at an illustration of locating a security flaw in an IPv4 network:

Vulnerability: Web Server Vulnerability that Has Not Been Patched

Scenario: A web application platform that is older than the organization's web server is used. This version has been found to include a bug that permits remote code execution.

Steps:

1. **Network Discovery**: Find the IP address of the web server using a network scanner (for example, 192.168.0.62).

2. **Vulnerability Scanning:** Apply a vulnerability scanner to the IP address of the web server. The scanner finds that an outdated web application platform with a known remote code execution vulnerability is being used by the web server.

3. **Penetration Testing:** Conduct a penetration test to take advantage of the weakness. Attempt to ethically run remote code on the web server. The severity of the vulnerability is demonstrated through successful exploitation.

4. **Patch and Update Management:** Look for updates or patches that fix the vulnerability on the vendor's website. Download and install the web server fix.

5. **Security Configurations**: Examine the firewall and security settings on the web server. Make sure access controls are configured appropriately and that only relevant ports are open.

6. **Monitoring and Intrusion Detection:** To keep an eye on the web server's behavior, set up intrusion detection. If an intrusion is successful, the company can react right away.

It's crucial to remember that IPv4 networks are equally susceptible to flaws like weak passwords, improperly configured services, a lack of encryption, and insufficient access controls. To reduce these risks, regular security audits and a strong cybersecurity plan are necessary.

9.7.2: Best practices for securing IPv4 networks

Implementing a variety of best practices to guard against potential attacks and vulnerabilities is necessary to secure IPv4 networks.

The Following are some essential guidelines to consider:

1. **Strong Access Controls:** Limit who has access to the network and its resources by implementing stringent access restrictions. To impose access restrictions based on IP addresses, ports, and protocols, use firewalls, routers, and access control lists (ACLs).

   Illustration: A corporation installs a firewall that restricts access to sensitive data-hosting servers to only a limited number of IP addresses from within the company's internal network. This stops outside parties who are not permitted to enter.

2. **Regular Patch Management:** Update all servers, software, and network equipment with the most recent security patches and upgrades. Older software frequently has known flaws that hackers can take advantage of.

Illustration: A business frequently checks its servers, switches, and routers for upgrades. They swiftly patch up security flaws with the most recent updates, lowering the chance of exploitation.

3. **Network Segmentation:** To reduce the possible impact of a security compromise, segment the network using VLANs or subnets. As a result, attackers cannot travel laterally within the network.

    Illustration: To protect important administration systems from illegal access, universities divide their student networks from their administrative networks.

4. **Encryption:** To safeguard data while it is being transmitted, use encryption methods like HTTPS, VPNs, and encrypted tunnels. This stops data interception and eavesdropping.

    Illustration: When a consumer checks out on an online store, their personal and financial information is protected using HTTPS encryption, making it more difficult for hackers to access the information.

5. **Intrusion Detection and Prevention:** Use intrusion detection and prevention systems (IDPS) to automatically stop or mitigate attacks by scanning network traffic for suspicious patterns or activity.

    Illustration: A business installs an IDPS that, upon detecting repeated failed login attempts, immediately blocks the source IP address, shielding its servers against brute-force attacks.

6. **User Authentication and Authorization:** To guarantee that only authorized users can access network resources, implement strict password regulations and multi-factor authentication.

    Illustration: Customers using an online banking platform are required to log in using a password and a one-time verification code that is given to their registered mobile device, adding an extra degree of security.

7. **Logging and Monitoring:** Establish logging and monitoring systems to keep tabs on network activity. Review logs frequently to spot potential security problems or odd patterns.

    Illustration: A business sets up logging on its firewalls and routers to keep track of all connection attempts. Every week, they review the logs to look for any unwanted access attempts.

8. **Educating Users:** Inform users and staff members about security best practices, such as how to spot phishing emails and when not to share sensitive information.

    Illustration: An organization regularly provides its staff with cybersecurity awareness training to inform them of the dangers of clicking on dubious links in emails and the significance of good password hygiene.

9. **Documentation:** Keep current records of your network's structure, configurations, and security guidelines. This facilitates troubleshooting and guarantees continuity throughout employee changes.

Illustration: An organization records the IP allocations, VLAN configurations, and firewall rules that make up its network architecture. The documentation makes it easier for the new engineer to comprehend the network setup if a network engineer departs the firm.

You can greatly improve your IPv4 network's security and lessen potential threats and vulnerabilities by adhering to these best practices and customizing them to meet the unique demands of your business.

9.7.3: Network monitoring and maintenance strategies

Strategies for network monitoring and upkeep are crucial for guaranteeing a network's dependability, efficiency, and security. These tactics entail continuously observing network activity, spotting faults, and taking proactive measures to stop or fix errors.

Here is a summary with an illustration:

Strategies for Monitoring a Network

1. **Real-Time Monitoring:** To acquire and analyze network data in real-time, use monitoring tools. This helps in the early detection of anomalies, snags, and security breaches.

2. **Performance Monitoring:** Keep track of important performance indicators including response times, latency, and packet loss. Performance monitoring assists in spotting and resolving performance degradation before it has an impact on consumers.

3. **Security Monitoring:** To keep an eye out for malicious activity and unauthorized access attempts, use intrusion detection systems

(IDS) and intrusion prevention systems (IPS). Examine network traffic patterns and logs to look for possible security vulnerabilities.

4. **Traffic Analysis:** To find patterns, trends, and potential bottlenecks, analyze network traffic. This aids in network resource optimization and capacity planning.

Strategies for Network Maintenance

1. **Regular Updates:** To address vulnerabilities and enhance performance, keep network devices, such as routers, switches, and firewalls, updated with the most recent firmware, patches, and security upgrades.

2. **Patch Management:** Create a patch management procedure to make sure software updates are applied consistently and on schedule. To reduce interruption, plan maintenance windows.

3. **Configuration Management:** Keep track of network device configurations in a single location. Review and update configurations frequently to make sure they comply with security guidelines and practical needs.

4. **Backup and Recovery:** Backup important data, switch configurations, and network device configurations frequently. In the event of failures or setup issues, having backups guarantees speedy recovery.

Illustration:

Monitoring: A financial institution uses specialized tools to implement real-time network monitoring. They observe a sharp rise in data flow outside of office hours. After further research, they found malware that was trying to exfiltrate important/sensitive customer data. They can find and stop the breach because of the monitoring system before any serious damage is done.

Maintenance: A configuration management solution is used by a big multinational company to keep track of the network devices and configurations. They discovered that some switches' firmware was out of date during routine reviews. To avoid potential security flaws and enhance network speed, the IT team plans a maintenance window during which the firmware will be updated.

Organizations may make sure that their networks are available, performant, and secure by putting in place efficient network monitoring and maintenance policies. A stable and dependable network environment is facilitated by regular monitoring and preventative maintenance

Review Exercise

4. A computer specialist made a variety of adjustments to fix the issue. A solution was eventually discovered after some unsuccessful attempts at solving the issue. What needs to be documented?

    A. Only the unsuccessful attempts, so that aspiring technicians can understand what to avoid trying.

B. A breakdown of the issue and its resolution.

C. Only the remedy since it addressed the issue.

D. All that was done to fix the issue.

Explanation

Documenting both the issue and its resolution is essential for several reasons:

- ✓ It provides a comprehensive record for future reference, allowing technicians to understand the problem and its solution.
- ✓ It facilitates knowledge transfer within the team, ensuring that everyone is aware of the issue and how it was resolved.
- ✓ It helps in troubleshooting similar issues in the future by providing insights into what worked and what didn't.
- ✓ It serves as a historical record for tracking trends or recurring problems, which can inform preventive measures.

While documenting unsuccessful attempts can be valuable for learning purposes, it's equally important to document the final resolution to provide a complete picture of the issue and its ultimate solution.

5. A network technician is troubleshooting an email connection problem. Which of the following end-user questions will provide clear information to better define the problem?

   A. What sort of technology do you employ to deliver emails?

B. When did you discover your email issue?

C. What is the Size of the emails you attempted to send?

D. Is your email operational right now?

Explanation

"When did you discover your email issue?" This question will help the technician understand the timeline of when the problem began, potentially identifying any recent changes or events that could be related to the email connection problem.

6. A networked PC can print to a nearby printer and ping other nearby computers, but it has problems connecting to the Internet. There are no problems with other PCs connected to the same network. What is the problem?

   A. The connection between the switch to which the PC is connected and the default gateway route is broken.

   B. The switchport's specified IPv4 address is wrong.

   C. There is no default route for the default gateway router.

   D. The computer's default gateway is either missing or incorrect.

   Explanation

   The computer's default gateway is either missing or incorrect. This scenario indicates that the PC can communicate within the local network (printing to a nearby printer and pinging other nearby computers) but cannot access the internet, suggesting an issue with its gateway configuration.

Chapter 10: Future of IPv4 and IPv6

The constraints of the established IPv4 protocol have grown more obvious as the demand for linked devices, online services, and data transport increases. As a result, IPv6—the next-generation protocol—was created to address the impending exhaustion of IPv4 addresses while providing a variety of improvements, such as a greatly increased address space and enhanced security features

IPv4 Exhaustion

When the internet was still in its infancy, IPv4, the fourth version of the Internet Protocol, was created. It was based on a 32-bit addressing scheme and could support a maximum of 4.3 billion distinct IP addresses. The pool of IPv4 addresses is quickly running out due to the fast growth of connected devices, including smartphones, tablets, IoT devices, and more. Due to the limited supply of IPv4 addresses, NAT solutions have become increasingly popular, allowing numerous devices on a private network to share a single public IPv4 address. While NAT has temporarily relieved some of the burden on the shrinking IPv4 address pool, it also adds complications, hinders end-to-end communication, and makes some network applications more difficult.

As the replacement for IPv4, IPv6 was introduced to address these issues. With a 128-bit addressing mechanism used by IPv6, there are an incredibly large number of unique addresses available—roughly 340 undecillion, to be exact. We won't run out of addresses anytime soon because of this enormous address space. By including features like stateless address autoconfiguration, IPv6 also combines improved security features and streamlines network configuration.

Due to the enormous size and complexity of the current internet infrastructure, the migration from IPv4 to IPv6 has been sluggish. Dual-stack networks, which enable devices and services to interact using both IPv4 and IPv6 protocols concurrently, are being implemented by many internet service providers, tech firms, and organizations. With this strategy, a seamless migration route and backward compatibility are guaranteed. The usage of IPv6 has increased as a result of growing awareness of its advantages in terms of scalability, security, and effective address distribution.

To ensure the internet's continued growth and sustainability, IPv6 has been adopted as a critical fix for IPv4's present expiration. Even though migration from IPv4 to IPv6 has its difficulties, it is an essential step in the development of a more interconnected and robust digital world. Collaboration between ISPs, IT businesses, and the larger online community will be crucial while the shift takes place to fully utilize IPv6 and influence the future of internet communication.

Reasons for IPv6 adoption

The limitations of IPv4 and the requirement for a more robust and efficient internet infrastructure are the primary drivers of IPv6 adoption. The following are the reasons for the adoption:

1. Address Exhaustion: The impending depletion of IPv4 addresses is the most pressing and obvious motivating cause. There are just not enough IPv4 addresses to handle the growing number of

connected devices. A long-term answer to this problem is provided by IPv6's enormous address space, which makes sure that the internet can continue to handle the expanding number of devices for years to come.

2. IoT Growth: The adoption of IPv6 has been significantly influenced by the Internet of Things (IoT) and its explosive expansion. To connect over the internet, IoT devices such as industrial sensors and smart home appliances need special IP addresses. To support the growth of these devices without turning to complicated workarounds like NAT, IPv6's large address space is crucial.

3. End-to-End Connectivity: With IPv6, devices can speak to one another directly without the assistance of Network Address Translation (NAT), reintroducing the idea of end-to-end communication. This is especially important for real-time communication (VoIP) and other applications that profit from direct connections, such as peer-to-peer networking, online gaming, and VoIP. Network setups are made easier and user experiences are improved with the move away from NAT.

4. Security Enhancements: Built-in security measures in IPv6 include the requirement for IPsec capability, which offers authentication and encrypted communication. Security is prioritized in IPv6 by design, in contrast to IPv4, where capabilities like IPsec are optional and frequently not widely used. In the current threat

environment, when cyberattacks are a continual worry, this is extremely crucial.

5. Global Standards and Regulations: Numerous governmental agencies and business associations have acknowledged the significance of IPv6 adoption. To encourage the switch to IPv6, certain nations and regions have implemented rules or incentives. Organizations are motivated to embrace IPv6 by a combination of legal compliance and a desire to adhere to international standards.

6. Future-Proofing Networks: The demand for a future-proof internet infrastructure grows as the technological landscape changes. Because of its large address space and built-in support for contemporary networking requirements, IPv6 is positioned as a solution that can handle future advancements in technology.

7. Service Provider and Industry Support: A significant number of internet service providers (ISPs), IT companies, and cloud service providers have actively promoted IPv6 adoption. This concerted effort from major enterprises in the sector pushes other businesses to copy it as IPv6 becomes a requirement for maintaining competitiveness and offering cutting-edge internet services.

IPv6 Features

The Internet Protocol version 6 (IPv6) offers several features and advantages that help move the digital world closer to a connected and secure future. IPv6 marks a fundamental development in the way devices communicate over the internet. IPv6 not only eliminates the address shortage but also paves the way for cutting-edge technologies like the Internet of Things (IoT) and next-generation communication networks like 5G thanks to its large address space, strong security features, and improved routing.

The following are the comparative features of IPv4 and IPv6

No	Features	IPv4	IPv6
1.	Address Size	Uses 32-bit addresses, with a maximum number of 4.3 billion possible addresses.	Uses 128-bit addresses, offering a vastly expanded address space with room for almost 340 undecillion distinct addresses.
2.	Address Notation	Addresses are expressed in dotted-	Hexadecimal addresses are formatted as 2001:0db8:85a3:0000:0000:8a2e:037 0:7334, with colons used to separate

		decimal format, with each octet represented by a decimal digit (for example, 192.168.0.1).	them. Leading zeros within each segment can be removed for clarity's sake.
3.	Address Configuration	Typically assigns addresses to devices by manual configuration or DHCP (Dynamic Host Configuration Protocol).	Supports either DHCPv6 for more complex configuration or stateless address autoconfiguration, where devices can create their addresses based on network prefixes and MAC addresses.

4.	Address Types	Comprises unicast, broadcast, and multicast addresses primarily.	Introduces the concepts of unicast, multicast, and anycast addresses. Anycast addresses enable numerous devices to share a single address, often forwarding traffic to the closest device.
5.	Network Address Translation (NAT)	NAT is commonly used because of its capacity to address shortages. It enables the sharing of a single public IP address among devices connected to a private network.	Due to the large address space, which encourages end-to-end communication and eliminates the need for complicated NAT installations, NAT is less common.

6.	Routing and Subnetting	To handle address exhaustion, subnetting is crucial, and CIDR, or Classless Inter-Domain Routing supports a range of subnet sizes.	Subnetting is still vital, but the large address space reduces the need for frequent readdressing and promotes easier subnet allocation.

Dual-stack network concept

A basic strategy utilized to make the switch from the IPv4 protocol to the more recent IPv6 protocol is the idea of a dual-stack network. It entails letting network devices connect while simultaneously executing the IPv4 and IPv6 protocols on those devices. This strategy guarantees a seamless transition phase during which devices can communicate using any protocol that is supported by both parties.

An explanation of the dual-stack network idea is provided below:

1. **Running Both IPv4 and IPv6**: Devices are set up to support both IPv4 and IPv6 in a dual-stack network. A device thus

contains two different stacks of networking protocols—one for IPv4 and the other for IPv6. Due to the availability and compatibility of the other device, the device can now communicate using either protocol.

2. **Transition Period**: Numerous networks, services, and gadgets will continue to largely use IPv4 during the IPv4 to IPv6 transition. In the interim, some more recent devices and services will employ IPv6. Devices in these mixed contexts can interact without any issues thanks to the dual-stack technique.

3. **Addressing**: An IPv4 address and an IPv6 address are both assigned to devices in a dual-stack network. The sending device determines whether the destination device supports IPv6 before delivering data to it. If it does, the sender device communicates using its IPv6 address. The sender device uses its IPv4 address if the recipient device is IPv6 incompatible.

4. **Router Configuration**: A dual-stack network's routers are set up to enable IPv4 and IPv6 routing. Both IPv4 and IPv6 traffic are managed by them, with IPv4 traffic being sent to IPv4 devices and IPv6 traffic being sent to IPv6 devices.

5. **Application Layer Compatibility**: Applications running on hardware connected to a dual-stack network must support both IPv4 and IPv6. Making sure the application can function with both IP address types and communicate using either protocol entails this.

6. **Gradual Transition**: The dual-stack method enables a smooth migration from IPv4 to IPv6. The network can progressively switch more of its traffic to IPv6 as more devices and services begin to support IPv6, while still being compatible with devices that solely support IPv4.

7. **Simplifying Transition Mechanisms**: Dual-stack networks can make it easier to develop transitional methods that help transfer IPv6 traffic over IPv4 networks, such as tunneling techniques. In an environment where IPv4 predominates, these strategies can be utilized to guarantee connectivity between IPv6 islands.

When switching from IPv4 to IPv6, the dual-stack strategy offers a workable way to ensure connectivity and compatibility. As IPv6 use rises, it enables network administrators to manage the coexistence of the two protocols while converting their infrastructure and services over time.

IPv4 to IPv6 gradual migration strategies

The transition from IPv4 to IPv6 is a complicated process that requires careful planning to achieve minimal disruptions and maximum compatibility. Here are a few strategies for a seamless and steady migration:

1. **Dual-Stack Implementation**: Configure hardware, routers, and services to support IPv4 and IPv6 at the same time. This enables devices to communicate using any available protocol. Devices can function in mixed IPv4 and IPv6 settings during the smooth transition phase.

2. **Priority-Based Migration**: Determine which crucial programs, services, or applications need IPv6 support. Prioritize migrating these systems first to guarantee that crucial functions can run without interruption in the new setting.

3. **New Deployments in IPv6**: Consider directly implementing new services on IPv6 whenever you're setting them up. This strategy expedites the development of your IPv6 network by preventing the buildup of new IPv4-dependent systems.

4. **IPv6-Only Subnets**: Declare a portion of your network to only support IPv6. This strategy promotes the use of IPv6 and enables you to separate IPv6-related difficulties from problems with your IPv4 infrastructure.

5. **Testing and Staging**: For your IPv6 migration, create a testing and staging environment. Before making modifications to the production network, this environment enables you to test the interoperability of apps, gadgets, and services in a private context.

6. **Gradual Service Transition**: One at a time, migrate services from IPv4 to IPv6. To develop practice and confidence in IPv6 operations, start with non-critical services. Advance to more crucial services as your proficiency increases.

7. **Vendor and Provider Collaboration**: Ensure that service providers and vendors support IPv6 by working together. To ensure a smooth transfer, confirm that your hardware, software, and third-party services are IPv6 compatible.

8. **Education and Training**: Introduce IPv6 concepts, configurations, and troubleshooting to your IT personnel and admins. The difficulties of moving can be handled more skillfully by a knowledgeable team.

9. **Monitoring and Testing Tools**: Use monitoring programs that can keep track of IPv4 and IPv6 performance. Test and monitor the network frequently to find problems and guarantee peaceful coexistence.

10. **Address Planning**: To ensure effective address space utilization and prevent conflicts, provide a comprehensive IPv6 address plan that includes subnetting and allocation.

11. **Gradual Decommissioning**: Consider phasing down IPv4 hardware and services gradually as IPv6 acceptance rises. However, keep in mind that due to legacy dependencies, complete IPv4 retirement may not be possible soon.

12. **Engage with Industry Groups**: Join organizations and industry groups devoted to IPv6 to get knowledge from others' experiences and insight into best practices

Keep in mind that the transition to IPv6 is a lengthy process, and the strategies you select should be in line with the requirements, capabilities, and objectives of your firm. A well-articulated migration plan will aid in making the changeover seamless while retaining operational integrity.

Review Exercise

1. Given IPv6 address 2001: ABCD: CAFE:100::1/64, what will be the network address?

   A. 2001: :/64

   B. 2001: ABCD: :/64

   C. 2001: ABCD: CAFE:100: :/64

   D. 2001: ABCD: CAFE: :/64

   Explanation

   IPv6 addresses consist of 128 bits, typically represented in hexadecimal format and divided into eight groups of 16 bits each, separated by colons. The "/64" in the address indicates that the first 64 bits represent the network portion of the address, and the remaining 64 bits are for host addressing.

   In the given IPv6 address "2001: ABCD: CAFE:100::1/64", the first 64 bits are "2001: ABCD: CAFE: 100:". This portion represents the network address because it encompasses the network identifier and subnet identifier.

   So, the network address is "2001: ABCD: CAFE:100: :/64". All devices within this network share the same network prefix, and the last 64 bits of the IPv6 address can be used for host addressing within that network.

2. A device with network interfaces capable of initiating and comprehending both IPv4 and IPv6 packets is referred to as?

   A. Dual-stack

   B. Tunnel

C. Port forwarding

D. Encapsulation

Explanation

Dual-stack refers to a networking configuration in which a device is capable of both initiating and comprehending both IPv4 and IPv6 packets. This allows the device to operate in networks that use either IPv4 or IPv6 protocols, ensuring compatibility and smooth communication across different types of networks.

About the Author

Am an expert in knowledge empowerment with substantial training and teaching experience in information, communication, and technology. I possess an array of experiences that I apply to my professional career. These include positions such as Oracle Academy Instructor, Cisco Systems Academic Instructor, Certified Lead Trainer, and ICDL Trainer of Trainers. My unwavering devotion to sharing information propels me beyond the boundaries of traditional education. With my unmatched teaching abilities, I expertly guide students through the complexity of technology, delivering precision and clarity. Many people follow in my footsteps, earning the knowledge and confidence required to pass certification exams and excel in their respective areas. My influence extends well beyond the classroom. As an examiner and IT practitioner for managed services, I carefully assess the changing environment of skills, ensuring that my guidance remains at the forefront of industry standards. With a diverse background that encompasses end-user computing, system administration, programming, and database management, I shape the goals of young professionals, molding them into competent experts in their respective fields. My passion for sharing information goes beyond the boundaries of conventional teaching methods. I exemplify the pinnacle of IT expertise, seamlessly blending conceptual understanding with practical implementation. I strive to provide my customers with a true sense of joy and purpose as they work toward realizing their goals.

Acknowledgment

In honor of my dear family

For the countless hours spent on this book's research, writing, and editing as well as for your continued support, inspiration, and understanding. I've always been inspired by your love and patience.

In honor of my dear clientele

I appreciate your trust in entrusting me with your networking requirements

and difficulties. These pages' insights have been influenced by your queries, comments, and practical experiences. To serve you is a privilege.

All of you have my sincere gratitude and appreciation as I dedicate this book to you

www.ingramcontent.com/pod-product-compliance
Lightning Source LLC
Chambersburg PA
CBHW071237050326
40690CB00011B/2162